Joe Namath

by JOHN DEVANEY

Illustrated with photos

SCHOLASTIC BOOK SERVICES
NEW YORK · TORONTO · LONDON · AUCKLAND · SYDNEY · TOKYO

Material for this book came from many sources, including a number of interviews I have had with Joe Namath for *Sport* Magazine and Fawcett *Football Yearbooks*. I am indebted to a number of books on Joe, especially these: Joe's autobiography written with Dick Schaap, *I Can't Wait Until Tomorrow*; *Countdown to Super Bowl* by Dave Anderson; and *Joe Namath's Sportin' Life*, by Maury Allen. — J.D.

PHOTO CREDITS
Page 4, UPI; page 18, NEA; pages 24, 29, Beaver Falls Tribune; page 44, University of Alabama; page 51, UPI; page 64, Ken Regan, Camera 5; page 72, Dan Sterbling, Camera 5; page 77, Wide World; pages 89, 101, 111, UPI; pages 118, 131, 140, Wide World; page 151, UPI; page 154, Ken Regan, Camera 5; page 157, UPI.

This book is sold subject to the condition that it shall not be resold, lent, or otherwise circulated in any binding or cover other than that in which it is published — unless prior written permission has been obtained from the publisher — and without a similar condition, including this condition, being imposed on the subsequent purchaser.

Copyright © 1972 by John Devaney. All rights reserved. Published by Scholastic Book Services, a division of Scholastic Magazines, Inc.

1st printing .... October 1972

Printed in the U.S.A.

CONTENTS

Joe Comes Back	5
The Choice for Joe	15
The $400,000 Quarterback	36
He'd Make It — One Way or the Other	55
Is Joe Namath Quitting?	71
How To Be a Leader	85
"On to the Super Bowl...."	99
Joe Guarantees It	116
"You did it, boy...."	126
Joe Comes Home	144
Appendix:	
Joe Namath's Record	160

Joe tosses a pass for fun in California. He went to Hollywood to make a film after the Jets' 1969 Super Bowl victory.

Joe Comes Back

Jets Versus 49ers, 1971

THE HUGE CROWD in Shea Stadium began a rising roar. The Jet quarterback, Bob Davis, was being helped off the field after a slamming tackle by a San Francisco 49er; and the crowd was roaring its welcome to the man who would replace him — Joe Willie Namath.

Joe shucked off his green parka as he saw Davis hobbling off the field. "Aw, shoot," he said. There was no time to warm up his arm. And, in fact, he really wasn't ready to go into the game. It had been almost four months since he'd played "under heat," as the quarterbacks say, standing in the teeth of a pass rush. And out there, those 49ers, led by 250-

pound Cedrick (Nasty) Hardman, were unleashing the most brutal pass rush in their conference.

"Relax," Joe Willie said to himself as he walked slowly onto the field, hearing the excited roar of the fans. "Relax . . . relax . . . relax . . ." But inside he felt very nervous. He not only hadn't played a game in four months, but until two weeks ago he hadn't even *thrown* a football.

He walked in a stiff-legged way toward the waiting Jet huddle. A steel brace gripped each knee, firming the joints so that they wouldn't unhinge. Five times surgeons had repaired those knees, most recently only four months before, when Joe, trying to tackle a player in a meaningless preseason game, had torn ligaments in his left knee.

Besides that, almost a year before, a tackler had hit him and fractured his right wrist. Since then, the Jets had played nineteen regular-season games without their All-Pro quarterback.

But no one was thinking of this now — not Joe, nor the Jets, nor the 49ers, nor this crowd of 64,000 fans. What was important was that Joe Willie Whiteshoes had come back to play.

Joe ducked into the huddle. Watching him, big Jet tackle Winston Hill felt a surge of pride and hope. "Now, we're really in there," he thought, "with the best passer in football on our side."

Joe called a running play. "Let's go," he said. The Jets clapped hands and wheeled out of their huddle, coming to the line. The 49ers were leading, 7-0, midway through the second period.

Joe stood over center John Schmitt, scanning the 49ers' defense. He saw they were looking for a run, and he shouted out new signals, changing the play to a pass.

Joe took the snap from Schmitt. He stepped into the pocket, the pass rushers slamming into the Jet blockers, the crack of pads and the shouts of the players piercing the roar of the crowd. As Joe looked for lanky wide receiver Don Maynard, he thought a big 49er was about to crash down on him. Hastily Joe threw the ball. It fell short at Maynard's feet.

In the huddle Joe called another pass play. Again Joe thought he heard a 49er coming at him. He quickly threw the ball and again it bounced short.

Joe kicked at the ground in frustration

and anger at himself. He knew what was wrong. "I'm throwing too quick," he growled to a teammate. "I think I'm about to be tackled and I let the ball go too soon."

"You're not used to playing under the pressure of a pass rush," the player said. "Man, you've been away a full season from a regular season game. You're not ready."

"Relax," Joe told himself. "Relax."

In the third period the 49ers were leading 17-0. At one point Joe steered the Jets on a long drive to the goal line, but there a Jet fumbled. Still the team had confidence: their Joe Willie Whiteshoes would get them on the scoreboard.

Joe knew he had to score quickly. Time was running out. He stepped back into the pocket. He looked downfield. Richie Caster, his prime receiver, was racing down the sideline. Joe ignored the flailing arms and grasping hands of 49er pass rushers, who were trying to climb over blockers to smash him down. He waited, waited, then pegged the ball to a spot some fifty yards downfield. Caster raced for that spot, grabbed the ball, and ran into the end zone.

Touchdown! Shea Stadium erupted with a

sound like a million firecrackers exploding. The Jets, though trailing 17-7, were back in the ballgame. Every man, woman, and child in the packed park knew Joe Willie Namath wasn't through — yet. He'd throw for another touchdown, the Jet fans just knew it, and they waited with a sense of anticipation.

Instead, the 49ers scored near the end of the third period, and as the fourth period started the Jets trailed by the seemingly hopeless margin of 24-7. But Joe wasn't giving up. He mixed passes and runs as the Jets stormed to the San Francisco 31. Joe stepped back to pass. As Joe let the ball go, big 250-pound "Nasty" Hardman crashed into him, one big fist cracking into Joe's jaw.

Joe rolled on the ground, his hand reaching for his mouth. "Have I got all my teeth?" he wondered. They were all there. He looked up and saw the pass had been completed. Good, he thought, and jumped up. He said nothing to Hardman. It was Hardman's job, dumping the passer. Joe knew that.

Two plays later Joe told Richie Caster to run a post pattern, running down the sideline, then cutting toward the goalposts. Joe stepped back. Hardman lunged at him, but Joe stepped away, calmly watching Caster.

He saw Richie cut into the open. Joe threw, his rusty arm aching now, and he threw low. But Richie Caster reached down, grabbed the ball at his knees, and danced into the end zone. Another Jet touchdown. Now it was San Francisco 24, Jets 14.

"How about that Caster!" said a Jet coach at the sideline. "He's been dropping easy passes all season. Now he makes a great catch on a low one."

"It's because of Joe," another coach said. "Everybody's giving a little bit extra because they've got Joe out there. With Joe passing you know you've always got a chance to win."

Some two minutes later the ball sat on the San Francisco 22-yard line. Joe called for a pass. He looked toward the end zone and spotted Jet receiver Ed Bell, with a 49er defensive back about ten yards in front of him. Artfully, ever so carefully, Joe lobbed the ball over the back's helmet and into Ed Bell's hands. Touchdown! The score was 24-21, with some five minutes left to play — plenty of time for another Jet TD and a victory.

The crowd was roaring as the desperate 49ers clung to the ball for the next four minutes, making first downs to run out the clock. But finally the Jet defense held, forcing the

49ers to punt. Now the Jets had the ball on their 28, a long seventy-two yards from where they wanted it to be. Joe stalked onto the field, his face grim. He looked at the clock. It showed 1:31 to play.

Joe passed to Richie Caster for ten yards. He passed to Ed Bell for twenty-three yards. Now the Jets were at the San Francisco 39-yard line. The 49ers were looking for a pass, but Joe handed off to Emerson Boozer, who raced through the spread-out 49er defense and blasted to the San Francisco 19.

There were only sixteen seconds remaining. Joe, scanning the defense, noticed that safety man Johnny Fuller had been leaving the area to cover receivers cutting across the middle. Hastily, in the huddle, Joe told Richie Caster to cut across the middle. He hoped Fuller would leave the area to cover Caster. Then he told Ed Bell to cut into that area and look for a pass.

The crowd was standing, watching this last play, hoping they were going to see one of the season's biggest upsets. The 49ers had won seven games that season and led their division. The Jets had won only four.

Joe hut-hutted the quarterback's chant. He stepped back into the pocket. Big "Nasty"

Hardman and the other pass rushers pounded at his wall of blockers, screaming to distract Joe. Joe cocked the ball at his ear with both hands and looked downfield. He saw Caster cut across the middle. Good. Caster should have pulled the safety man, Fuller, with him. Joe saw Ed Bell cutting into the area.

Joe threw. He threw that ball with all the strength he had left in his aching arm. And as he sent the ball winging, Joe knew he'd thrown it perfectly, "the best pass I threw all day," he said later.

He saw the ball drill toward Bell. Then, suddenly, there was a white 49er jersey leaping at the goal line. It was Fuller! The 49er hadn't been fooled. He hadn't followed Caster; he hadn't left the area.

Fuller reached high into the air and plucked off the pass. He ran up field and was forced out-of-bounds. A pistol cracked, ending the game.

Big Cedrick Hardman walked over to the downcast Joe. Hardman stuck out his hand. "Joe," he said, "you were always my idol and you are still my idol."

Joe smiled, his teeth still aching from that blow by Hardman. In his soft drawl, Joe said, "I thank you sincerely."

The 49ers' quarterback, John Brodie, ran out to Joe. He draped a hand over Joe's back and told him how much the 49ers had admired Joe's courage in rallying the Jets for three touchdowns to almost win the game.

"He got us the fourth touchdown that would have won this game," a Jet player said to Brodie, "except we fumbled it away."

The Jet clubhouse was a mob scene. It looked like that day in 1969 when Joe had led the team to an upset victory in the Super Bowl. Someone was shouting out Joe's passing statistics for the game: three touchdown passes, 11 completions in 27 attempts for a gain of 258 yards — the greatest yardage gain by a Jet passer all season long.

Joe's dad rushed into the clubhouse. He embraced Joe. "Terrific!" he yelled. "You were terrific!"

Joe wasn't smiling at his father. He said simply, "We didn't win."

All his life Joe had been a winner: in high school in Beaver Falls, Pennsylvania; in college at the University of Alabama; and here in professional football. The Jets had been a team of also-rans until Joe passed the Jets to the Super Bowl championship. Once, sitting on a jet airliner, he turned to a sportswriter and said, "I've always been fortunate to be associated with winners."

Winning! It was always foremost in Joe's mind, even when he was having a good time away from football. The week before the Super Bowl game in Miami, he was sitting in a nightspot, enjoying a thick steak, cold drinks, and a lot of laughs. Then he met a Colt player, Lou Michaels, a Colt he would be playing against for the Super Bowl championship. Joe Willie Whiteshoes looked directly at Michaels and said seriously, "The Jets are going to win."

Joe was enjoying his good time on the town. But when it came time to play, he would be ready. Ready to win.

And the Jets, the underdogs of the game, did win, shocking the Colts and the nation, just as Joe Willie had promised they would. But this was Joe Namath's way — a winner doing the unexpected, a winner making the impossible dream come true. It had started when he was a boy back in Beaver Falls, Pennsylvania, when he proudly wore the number 19 of Johnny Unitas, and dreamed that one day he, Joe Namath, would be another Johnny U.

The Choice for Joe

THE SKINNY SOPHOMORE, only five feet tall, stood on tiptoe. He was trying to peer over the shoulders of other boys looking at a paper posted on a bulletin board. "Is my name up?" someone shouted.

"No," said a boy reading the list. He let out a whoop. "But mine is."

"And so is mine," shouted another boy.

The skinny sophomore slipped through the crowd to get a closer look. There were fifty names typed on the list — the names of boys attending Beaver Falls High School, who had been invited to come to a preseason training camp for the football team. Little Joe Namath, 110 pounds in his sneakers, had hoped his name might be on the list. Hadn't he been second-string quarterback for his junior high school team?

Joe scanned the list, but his name wasn't there. The coach evidently didn't want him on the team.

Joe turned away from the bulletin board, deeply disappointed. He really wanted to be a quarterback. His brother, John, had been the Beaver Falls quarterback ten years ago, and Joe wanted to be the second Namath to lead the Beaver Falls Panthers.

The boy wished he were as tall and strong as his other brother, Frank, who had been a speedy lineman there five years ago. Frank had gone on to the University of Kentucky. Joe remembered meeting the Kentucky football coach, Blanton Collier, who later became the coach of the Cleveland Browns. "How about you, little fella?" Collier had said to the thirteen-year-old Joe, ruffling his hair. "Are you going to play football?"

"Yes," Joe had answered, shyly.

"What position will you play?"

"Quarterback," Joe had said in a firm voice.

Joe lived with his father and mother at the lower end of Beaver Falls, Pennsylvania, a section of town where families, whose fathers worked in the steel mills, lived. Joe's father was a steel worker. One day, when Joe was nine or ten, his father took him into the mill where he worked. Little Joe stared wide-eyed at the clanging machinery, his eardrums pounded by the din, his skin warmed by the hot blast of the furnace. The boy wanted to run right out of there. He knew then that this was no place for him. When he grew older, Joe planned to be a baseball player, or football star, or a basketball champ. Through any sport — and Joe had a choice — he wanted to escape working in the steel mills.

For a young boy, Beaver Falls was a serene and beautiful place in which to live. The town of about 16,000 people was one of many little towns nestled in Beaver Valley not far from Pittsburgh, Pennsylvania. Joe fished, swam in the river, played ball with the boys of his neighborhood. One day he and a black friend, Linwood Alford, decided to walk across the rickety railroad trestle connecting Beaver Falls with the town of New Brighton. Suddenly, as they were picking their way across the trestle, the boys saw a train rattling

Joe as a boy growing up in Beaver Falls, Pennsylvania.

across the trestle — coming right at them. Joe and Linwood leaped for a railing and hung on, as the train roared by within a few feet of them.

With the other boys of the Lower End, Joe played all sports and made some up, like rock fights. Joe joked, years later, that throwing rocks as a boy was one reason he grew up with such a strong arm.

Joe was always bouncing a ball or tossing it to someone. Each morning his father, as he left for the steel mill, would see Joe playing catch with his sister Rita before they went to school. When Mr. Namath came home at night, he'd see Joe running toward his two older brothers, trying to dodge them, but they would knock him down, hitting him clean and hard. Joe always bounced right up, glad they were hitting him as though he were their equal.

One evening, as Joe's father got ready for dinner, he heard a thumping against the wall of another bedroom. He investigated and found Joe lobbing a softball against the wall.

"What do you think you're doing?" Joe's father demanded.

"I'm practicing my hook shot for basketball," Joe said.

Catch, football, basketball. And when Joe was nine, he trotted onto a field one day for Little League tryouts. That night the boy came home with a woeful look on his face. "Those other boys are much better than me," Joe said.

Joe's dad stared at the baseball uniform Joe was wearing. It was an old one of Frank's, cut down by his mother. "Well," his father said slowly, "you'd better give up your uniform then. If you don't have confidence, you can't do anything."

His father's comment made a strong impression. The next year Joe was roaming the outfield for his Little League team, running faster than any boy on the team. In one game, he hit a single. In another, he hit a single, a double, and a home run. "You're a good hitter, Joe," a friend said to him.

Joe grinned. He *knew* he was a good hitter. He could see every pitch coming toward him, as big as a melon. He could hit anybody, he told his father, who smiled, pleased that his son was building up the confidence he needed.

Joe tried out for the junior high school basketball team. He lobbed shots from fifteen and twenty feet away, sinking shot after shot. It almost seemed as if the hoop grew wider after each shot. He became the star of his team, a quick guard who could pop the ball in from almost anywhere inside the midcourt line.

As for football, when he tried out for quarterback in junior high school, he made the team as the second-string quarterback. He could throw long, hard passes to receivers. But when he was rushed during a game, Joe was so small that he couldn't see over the rushing linemen.

"If I was a little taller," Joe told his dad after one game, "I could see over those big linemen."

"Stick with it, Joe," his dad told him.

But how could a determined winner stick with football in high school, when his name was not even on the list of candidates for the preseason football camp? Maybe, Joe thought, he should stay with basketball and baseball, the two sports he was playing so well. Maybe he should give up football. Maybe, at only five feet and 110 pounds, he was too small for football.

Joe went to see the high school football coach, Bill Ross. He told Coach Ross he thought he would not even try out for the football team, that he would concentrate instead on practicing his outside shooting to get ready for the basketball season.

Coach Ross listened to Joe, reflectively rubbing his chin. He knew the boy was a good athlete, that he had been an excellent passer in junior high. All he needed was time to grow. The coach told Joe he wanted him to come out for the team.

Joe shrugged. He went home to discuss it with his father. "Go to practice every day," his dad told him. "Let the coaches know you want to play."

So Joe did just that. And finally they let him play. In the last game of the football season — for the *last play* of the season — Joe went into a game as a sub for a defensive back. The opposing team ran the other way with the ball, and that was the beginning and end of Joe Namath's first season in football.

Coach Larry Bruno studied the schedule. So far in this 1959 football season the Beaver Falls team had won only three games while losing five and tying one. Bruno, a new coach who had succeeded Bill Ross, was thinking about his quarterback, Rich Neidbala, a senior. Rich was a good quarterback but he'd be gone the next season. It was time for Bruno to decide who his next quarterback would be.

That boy Joe Namath was growing, thought the coach. He was — what? — five-foot-nine right now, and he seemed to grow an inch every time you looked at him.

Joe was now in his junior year at Beaver Falls High. Bruno had been impressed with Joe the first day he'd seen him throw a pass and hand off to a back. "He has inborn talent," Bruno told a friend. "Joe is one of those people who could pick up a ping-pong paddle for the first time in his life, and within a half hour would be the best ping-pong player in the room. He's the kind who will always be the best at everything he tries. When I show him something, I only have to show him once. Right away he gets the idea. And in a few days he is a master at it."

Bruno decided to start Namath at quarterback in the last game of this 1959 season. And the coach's hunch about Joe was right. The Beaver Falls Panthers routed New Brighton with Joe tossing several touchdown passes. To Joe's delight, the coach told him, "You're my starting quarterback for next season."

That winter Joe played basketball. In one

Joe, at 18, poses with costar Benny Singleton (left) of the Beaver Falls basketball team and coaches.

game Beaver Falls was losing by a point in the closing seconds of the game. The opposing team's rooters began to chant off the remaining seconds . . . *"seven . . . six . . . five . . . four . . ."*

Joe Namath was dribbling the ball some thirty feet from the basket . . . *". . . three . . . two . . ."*

Joe arched the ball toward the basket. He saw it spin through the air. Then Joe turned his back to the basket and pointed two fingers high into the air. He was telling this crowd that the ball was going to sail through the hoop for two points.

The ball swished through the nets for a Beaver Falls victory. Fans rushed onto the court and hoisted Joe Willie Namath high into the air. He was smiling. He'd just *known* that ball would go through the hoop, which had looked as big as a manhole cover when he let it go. His father's words, "You've got to have confidence in yourself," had stuck deep with Joe. He was brimming with confidence now.

In the spring of 1960 Joe trotted onto a baseball diamond in a Beaver Falls High uniform. That spring he pitched, played the infield and the outfield — every position except catcher. Mostly he raced over the outfield, spearing long drives. When runners tried to scamper from first to third on base hits, Joe made throws on a line to cut them down. At bat he dug his spikes into the batter's box, swishing the bat slowly through the air. He was even taller now, about five-foot-eleven, with ropelike arms and a muscled, compact, 170-pound body. He waited for the good pitch, then smacked hits between infielders, through the outfielders, and over the fences. A Chicago White Sox scout watched him one day and said, "A sure big leaguer."

Joe's mother and father were now divorced. Although Joe often saw his father, and they were on good terms, he continued to live with his mother. To earn money and help out at home, he found an after-school job as a caddy at a golf course. Whenever he could, Joe fished out a club from a player's bag and hit balls onto the greens. One day a man watched as Joe drilled ball after ball onto a green from 150 yards away.

"How long you been playing golf, son?" the man asked.

"A few months."

"I been playing golf for ten years and I

can't do that," the man said, a rueful smile on his face.

Joe didn't even know the names of the clubs, he was so new to the game. Once he and a friend were caddying. A golfer said to Joe's friend, "Give me my spoon."

His friend looked at Joe. Joe shrugged. He didn't know, any more than his friend did, that a spoon was a Number Three wood.

Joe's friend pulled club after club out of the bag, looking for a spoon. Then he turned the bag upside down, all the clubs tumbling out. Still no spoon.

Joe's friend turned to the goggle-eyed golfer. "There ain't no spoon in there," Joe's friend said. "But you wait here and I'll go back to the dining room and get one."

That summer Joe enjoyed himself. He fished in the Beaver River. He batted baseballs on the athletic fields around town. He swam in the town swimming pools. Beaver Falls was, as he often said years later, a nice place to grow up in.

One afternoon Joe went hunting with a friend. It was the first time that Joe had ever hunted. Joe saw a small bird circling over a tree. He lifted up his BB gun and pulled the trigger. The bird spun crazily in the air, then flopped to the ground like a stone. Joe ran over. He looked down at the bird, dying in front of him, and he never went hunting again.

"Is that little Joe Namath?" one Beaver Falls man asked another as they watched the team working out in the fall of 1960. "Joe was such a skinny little kid just a few years ago. He sure did grow fast." Joe Namath, the starting quarterback for the Panthers, was now a hefty five-foot-eleven, 175-pound senior.

At the start of the season Joe asked for and got the number 19, the number worn by his idol, Johnny Unitas, quarterback for the Baltimore Colts. Like Joe, Johnny Unitas was from a steeltown — nearby Pittsburgh. On television, Joe watched Unitas steer the Colts to victory after victory. Often, when Joe ducked back to pass during a scrimmage, he imagined he was Johnny U. looking for his favorite receiver, Raymond Berry.

Joe's crewcut was styled hairbrush-stiff like Johnny U's. Joe barked out plays in the confident, quick manner of Johnny U. And he worked at learning to "audible" the way Johnny U. could audible — that is, after scan-

Called "Joey U." because he wore Johnny Unitas' number 19 in high school, Joe runs 58 yards for a touchdown.

ning the defense, he changed the play at the line of scrimmage by calling out new signals. Some people in Beaver Falls began to call Joe Namath "Joey U."

With Joey U. throwing touchdown passes and switching plays at the line of scrimmage, Beaver Falls won its first game, beating Midland, 43-13. The next week Joey U. completed eight of nine passes, and the Beavers bowled over Sharon, 39-7.

"He's calling 99 percent of the plays out there," Coach Bruno said after the game. "I let him do it. I don't want to mess things up. I watch him out there, pausing at the line of scrimmage, and I know he's calling an audible. He can pick a defense apart."

In the Midland game Joe shoved a ball toward a fullback on a handoff play. The back dashed into the line and was piled up. The referee blew his whistle. Then the referee turned his head and saw the Beaver Falls halfback running with the ball down the sideline, on his way for a touchdown. Joe had faked the ball to the fullback, then handed off to the halfback, fooling both the opposition and the referee. After the game the referee said, "In fifteen years, I've never been fooled so often by a high school quarterback."

Beaver Falls next met New Castle, a school three times the size of Beaver Falls. Not in forty years had Beaver Falls ever defeated New Castle. Before the game, as Joe warmed up, Coach Bruno asked him: "How's your ankle? If we have to punt, you will have to do the punting."

"Don't worry, Coach," Joe said, confidence surging high inside him. "We're not going to have to punt."

He was right: Beaver Falls did not punt all evening long (its games were played on Friday nights at Geneva College Stadium). Early in the game Joe faked a handoff, then kept the ball himself and ran eight yards into the end zone for a touchdown. A little later he faked a handoff to his fullback, who crashed into the line; Joe pulled back the ball and gave it to halfback Bo Hayden who sprinted around end for a second touchdown. Joe threw a pass to his favorite receiver, end Tom (Krz) Krzmienski, for a third touchdown. He pitched out to halfbacks for two other touchdowns. He sneaked over from the six-inch line for another TD, and Beaver Falls had won its third straight, 39-0.

Word swept up and down the football-mad Valley, from Pittsburgh to Aliquippa. This

Joe Namath, this "Hungarian Howitzer," as the local newspapers called him, was a ball-handling magician and a long-touchdown passer. He was the best the Valley had seen since Babe Parilli, who had gone on to Kentucky to be an All-America.

Some 8,500 fans, nearly half the population of Beaver Falls, filled Geneva College Stadium for the Panthers' next game against a crack Ambridge team, rated the most powerful in the Valley. Fans gathered in clumps on the hill above the stadium, looking down at the lighted field glowing below.

Early in the game Joe was hit by a tackler, who twisted Joe's throwing arm. Joe left the game, holding the throbbing arm. He stayed out until only a minute was left in the first half, Ambridge ahead, 6-0.

Joe trotted back onto the field, the arm still sore. He took the ball and dropped back to his 30-yard line, looking for a receiver. He side-stepped one tackler, danced backward away from another. He saw Tom Krzmienski speeding down the sideline, covered by Ambridge's Fred Klages.

Klages, chasing Krzmienski, looked back and saw Namath start to throw from seemingly a mile away. "He can't throw this far,"

Klages thought. Klages turned to look for Krz. He saw the fifty-yard pass arching downward over Krz's helmet and into Krz's outstretched hands. Krz caught the ball on the Ambridge 35 and ran into the end zone for the first Panther touchdown. Beaver Falls was on its way to a 25-13 victory.

Beaver Falls went unbeaten that season, the team winning its first Western Pennsylvania championship in thirty-five years. Eleven players on that Beaver Falls team received college football scholarships and three later were given tryouts by the pros. All eleven finished four years of college. As Joe said years later, "We were fantastic."

That winter Joe also led the basketball team to a series of victories. But he argued with the coach, got angry during one game when the coach took him out of the game. Joe kept right on walking — right out of the arena. He never played basketball again for Beaver Falls. Years later Joe always said he'd been wrong to be angry with the coach.

In the spring he played baseball, hitting over .400 and pitching and batting the team to the Western Pennsylvania baseball championship. By mid-May of 1962 big-league baseball scouts and college football scouts were bumping into each other in the hallway outside Coach Bruno's office, wanting to sign Joe.

Like many boys of that time, Joe dressed in tight pants and sported a beret and dark sunglasses. It was groovy to dress that way. But some people in Beaver Falls began to criticize Joe for being too wild. One night he and some friends hoisted an orange-and-black balloon up the flag pole on a roof and were caught by the police. They were quickly released, but now in Beaver Falls people gossiped about "that bad boy Namath."

Joe's friend, Joe Tronzo, the sports editor of the Beaver Falls *News-Tribune*, later said. "There were crazy stories that Joe Namath brought a cow into the school auditorium; that he tried to bomb a school board member's house; and that the only thing he passed in high school was a football."

None of these stories was true, Joe Tronzo pointed out. Other than the balloon prank, Joe never had any trouble with the police. He had maintained close to C grades — not good, but all right for someone like Joe who never studied very hard. He had missed only one day of high school in three years — a day he had been excused.

But some college scouts frowned when they saw Joe's low grades. "You should have studied harder," Joe's mother often told him. "Then you could pick any college you liked."

"You're right," Joe told his mother for the thousandth time, knowing indeed that she was right.

Joe, however, began to wonder if he should go to college. The big-league scouts were offering him as much as $20,000 in bonus money to play baseball. One day Joe said to his father, "I'd have to shine a lot of shoes down at the Lower End to make $20,000."

"Twenty thousand dollars is a lot of money to a working man like me," his dad told Joe. "But is it worth an education?"

The $400,000 Quarterback

If you think you are better, you are.
If you think you dare not, you won't.
If you like to win but you don't think you can,
It's almost a cinch you won't.

JOE NAMATH stared at the poem, which was posted on a bulletin board in the University of Alabama football team's dressing room. Around him players shouted as they dressed after practice. Joe read the poem a second time. He knew the author of the poem. It was Bear Bryant, Alabama's football coach. Bear Bryant was a tough coach who didn't like to lose. One Saturday his team lost a game that the Bear thought it should have won. "There's a team meeting tomorrow," he snarled after the game. "At four-thirty."

"Four-thirty Sunday afternoon?" a player asked.

"No," the Bear snapped. "Four-thirty in the morning. And you all had better be there, *hear*?"

Joe, turning away from the poem, thought how glad he was he'd come to the University of Alabama. He had agreed with his dad: He should concentrate on getting a college education and then choose between football and baseball. And he liked the idea of coming to a school in the South, away from those cold December winds that ripped through the Valley. Even now, in the warmth of a sunny October afternoon in Tuscaloosa, Alabama, Joe shivered as he remembered those frigid mornings when he'd wake up cold and dress hastily, beating his arms against his chest to warm up. Joe thought he was going to like tossing passes in the balmy South. He'd never enjoyed trying to pass with his numbed hands as stiff as sticks.

Right from the start Joe had liked Bear Bryant. Although Joe was only a freshman and couldn't play varsity football that year,

Bear had made Joe feel at home when Joe strolled over to the football field to watch the varsity practice. Joe was dressed in one of his snappy Beaver Falls outfits: checked coat, straw hat, and black wraparound sunglasses.

Other students, in gray jackets and Ivy League pants, swiveled their heads to stare at Joe's bizarre outfit. Some girls giggled behind his back. Joe tried to ignore them, but no one likes to be laughed at. He was glad when he saw the Bear, standing atop a platform from where he could oversee the practice, wave to him. Joe waved back. The Bear invited Joe to climb up a ladder to the top of the platform and stand beside him.

"Who's that?" asked a reporter, watching Joe climb up the ladder with one hand while holding onto his straw hat with the other.

"That's Joe Namath," said an Alabama football fan. "He's a new freshman quarterback. And he must be good. That's the first time I ever saw the Bear invite a freshman up to the tower. He doesn't usually invite even a varsity letterman up there."

"Doesn't look much like a football player to me," said someone else. "Not in that getup he's wearing."

Joe found out he was different from other

students in more ways than his clothing. Joe disagreed with a number of the other students on racial matters. When the students talked about equal rights for blacks and whites, for instance, Joe defended people like Dr. Martin Luther King, who had started a boycott of buses by blacks in nearby Birmingham. Dr. King had told blacks not to ride the buses if they were forced to ride in the rear. Many of the Alabama football players, who had been raised in the South, thought Dr. King was causing needless trouble.

Joe didn't think so. And he said so. He had grown up with blacks in Beaver Falls. When he played for the Beaver Falls High School basketball team, Joe was the only white on the starting team. Some of the football players heard about that; they began to call Joe "nigger."

"I don't mind what you call me," Joe told them with his amiable, sleepy-eyed grin. "But I don't tell you what to think. You shouldn't try to make me think your way by calling me names. I like all you guys, but I don't agree with you when you say those things about blacks."

Some of the players wouldn't talk to him. Joe felt more and more alone. He missed the laughter and the noisy horseplay of his evenings back in Beaver Falls, when he met his friends to play pool or bowl or ride down to the river bank in old cars.

He began to feel like a trapped animal in his dorm at the University of Alabama. He knew nobody. He thought people looked at him strangely: the swarthy-faced Hungarian Catholic boy from Yankeeland. He thought the girls laughed at him and the boys scorned him. He felt so lonely he couldn't study. Sometimes he thought about running right out the door and keeping on running until he got back to his mother's house in Beaver Falls. Each night, looking out his window at the dark campus, he thought how much darker and creepier it seemed here than did the nights back in lively Beaver Falls.

Joe began to think about those baseball offers. A Baltimore Oriole scout had come to the campus and offered him a $50,000 bonus if he would quit football and sign a baseball contract. Joe said he would consider it.

The University of Alabama football coaches heard Joe was thinking about leaving school. "Let's get Bubba Church to talk to him about what life is really like in baseball," one assistant coach said.

Bubba Church had pitched for the Philadelphia Phillies in the 1950s. Now retired and living in Birmingham, he was friendly with the Alabama coaches. One day Bubba came to the campus and walked over to see Joe in his dormitory room.

"Hey, Joe," the cheerful Bubba said. "I understand you're thinking about quitting school and playing baseball for the Orioles."

"I've thought about it some," Joe said.

"Look, Joe, they'll give you a $50,000 bonus and you'll blow that in two years. You know you will. Then suppose your arm goes bad. Every player knows that can happen — at any time. Then what have you got? No college degree. Nothing."

Joe nodded, listening. Maybe Bubba was right. Maybe he ought to stay in college. He decided to stick it out for a while. And, as often happens, he found people he liked. Joe became pals with Mike Bite, a former manager of the football team, and with Jimmy Walsh, a laughter-loving prelaw student. Walsh and Bite were like the friends he'd known back in Beaver Falls. Soon they were buddies, going on triple dates with co-eds, seeing movies, or throwing darts in games that sometimes went on until dawn.

Joe also started to trade jokes with the 'Bama football players, and soon the good-humored Namath wit had won him friends among the other players. Once, during spring practice in 1962, Joe was working out with the varsity, although he was still a freshman. In the huddle Joe looked at the other players and said, "All right, old Joe is carrying the ball on this play. Let's see some blocking because I don't think old Bear wants me to get hurt."

The other players burst out laughing. But, in truth, Bear didn't want Joe to be hurt. At the start of the 1962 season, Namath was the Bear's starting quarterback, although Joe was only a sophomore. At first 'Bama fans protested. How come Bear was starting this Yankee sophomore instead of a Southern boy who was a senior? But they didn't protest too long. Not when they saw Joe flash that whiplike arm and toss long passes into the hands of receivers fifty yards downfield. Then they said, "Haven't seen a passer like that at 'Bama since Harry Gilmer way back around World War II."

Joe flipped 10 completions in 14 tries against Georgia in his first game. Three of those tosses were caught for touchdowns, Alabama winning, 35-0. Just like that, the sounds of the 'Bama fight song floating over the campus, Joe no longer was the strangely dressed kid from up North. He was the campus hero. Now the girls didn't giggle at Joe. They smiled at him, and every guy wanted to be his friend.

Alabama went on winning and soon was rated the Number One college team in the nation, winner of eight straight games. Georgia Tech came along to upset 'Bama, 7-6, but then Alabama overwhelmed Auburn, 38-0, and won an Orange Bowl bid to play against mighty Oklahoma on New Year's Day.

President John F. Kennedy watched that game, sitting in the sun in a brown stuffed chair. He saw Joe, early in the game, flip a twenty-five-yard pass into the end zone to a 'Bama receiver and Alabama led, 7-0. That really won the game. The Oklahoma Sooners were never able to pierce the 'Bama defense, and Joe led his team to two more scores and a 17-0 victory.

At the start of the 1963 season Joe and the other Alabama players were determined to avenge that one loss to Georgia Tech the year before. Alabama ran off another streak of victories, lost 10-6 to Florida, then came back

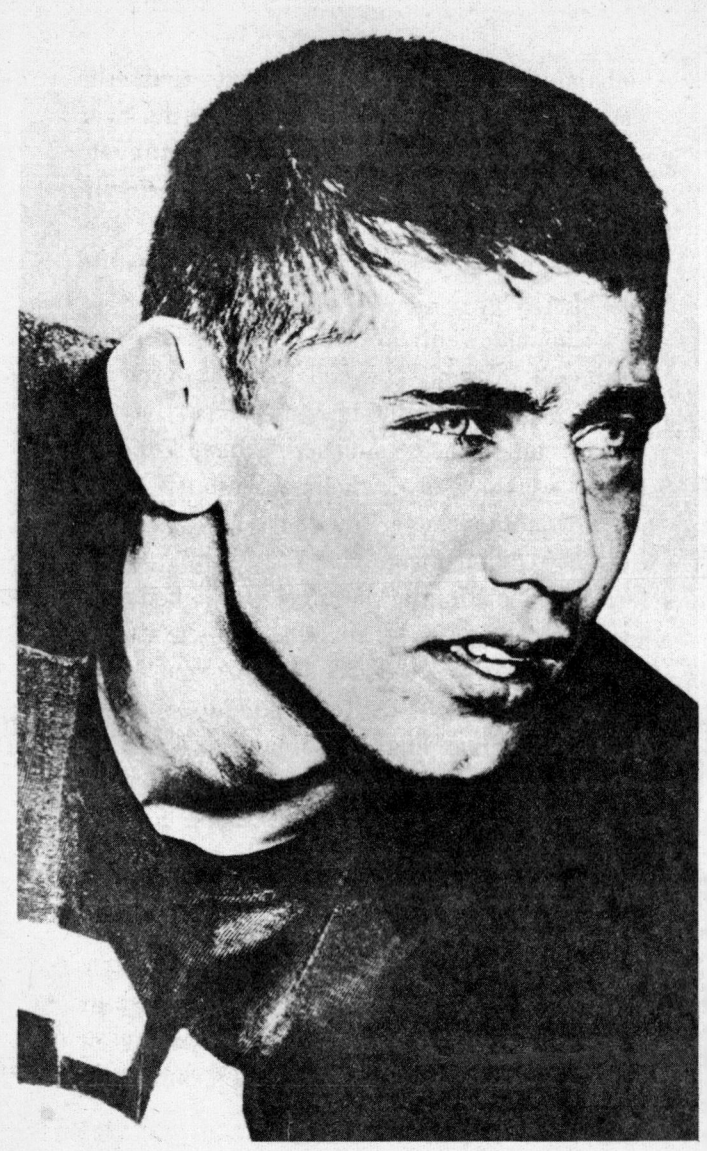

With crewcut, Joe poses during his junior year at Alabama.

to win three straight games. In an easy victory against Mississippi State, Joe fired 10 of 16 passes into the arms of his receivers.

"How come you can't stop those Namath passes?" an exasperated Mississippi State coach asked a defensive back during the game.

"He gets back and throws so quick," said the back, "that you haven't got time to cover a receiver. You see the receiver cut, you move toward him, and — *zip*! — before you've gone a half step, Namath's hit the receiver right in the hands."

Alabama now faced Georgia Tech, hoping to avenge that loss a year earlier. The eyes of the entire South were on the game. A worked-up Tech team drilled all week to stop those Namath passes, batting them down or intercepting them. The Tech coaches spread out the Tech defense to cover all of Namath's receivers.

Joe, crouching over his center at the start of the game, scanned the defense. He saw how it was spread. He handed off to a fullback. On the next play he pitched out to a halfback. The 'Bama backs ran straight through the spread-out Tech defense, gaining fifteen, twenty, and twenty-five yards a dash.

Joe threw only three passes all afternoon as Alabama won easily, 27-11. "Joe called such a smart game," the Bear said later, "that my assistants kept telling me not to mess him up by sending in any plays."

A few days after that victory, Joe went out after dark with some of his friends. They went to a party, and everyone had a good time, lots of laughs. Joe knew going to parties was breaking training rules, but just this one time . . .

Coach Bryant heard about the party. A few days later, Joe entered the team's dining room. He saw Coach Bryant. "Hey, Coach," Joe said, sitting down at the Bear's table, "I have some ideas for what we can do next week against . . ."

"Wait, Joe," the Bear said softly. "I think we'd better stop by my room a moment."

"Sure, Coach," Joe said, puzzled.

In his room the Bear asked Joe about the party. Yes, Joe admitted, looking Bear right in the eyes, he had gone to the party. He had broken training rules. Joe didn't tell the Bear that other football players had been at the party.

A few days later Coach Bryant announced to the newspapers that Joe Namath was suspended from the team for breaking rules. He would not play in the final game against Miami. Nor would he play in the Sugar Bowl, where 'Bama had been invited to meet Mississippi on New Year's Day.

Alabama football fans blinked, shocked. How could Bear suspend his best player, the best quarterback in the country, from the Bowl game? Thousands of letters and wires rained in on the Bear: Forgive Joe, reinstate him for the Bowl game.

The Bear appeared on a statewide telecast to explain why he couldn't. Hundreds of thousands watched their TV screens as the Bear explained that if he allowed his star to break rules, he couldn't make the rest of the players obey those rules. Joe would not be allowed to play.

Reporters asked Joe how he felt. "The coach was 100 percent right," Joe said. "No," he added, "make that 110 percent right."

Joe sat on the bench for the final game and watched his teammates beat Miami. And he was still on the bench, watching, as 'Bama beat Mississippi, 12-7, in the Sugar Bowl.

The Bear reinstated Joe for the 1964 season. Missing a Sugar Bowl game, Bryant decided, was punishment enough for Joe. Again the Alabama Crimson Tide rolled over opponents, winning their first game, their second game, their third game, their fourth game . . . Headlines across the country told the same story week after week:

NAMATH PASSES 'BAMA TO VICTORY

Opposing players began to needle Joe about his fame. "Hey, number 12," a Vanderbilt player yelled at Joe after tackling him, "what's your name?"

"You'll see it in the headlines tomorrow," Namath said with a sly grin. Joe was right. The next day's headlines read: Namath Passes Down Vanderbilt, 24-0.

Other players kidded Joe about his habit of wrapping white adhesive tape around his shoes. Joe liked to run with the ball in those flashy all-white shoes. The players began to call him Joe Willie Whiteshoes. They said he couldn't carry the ball if he wasn't wearing those white shoes. "I'll show you," Joe told them before a game against North Carolina State. "This game I won't tape my shoes."

Early in the game Joe rolled out to his right. He stopped, intending to cut back to his left. Suddenly his right knee collapsed under him. Joe collapsed on the grass, his face twisted with pain.

An ambulance sped him to a hospital. There, while his teammates were defeating North Carolina State, Joe learned he had torn cartilage in the knee. Joe saw the knee puffing up. He gritted his teeth as doctors inserted needles into the knee to drain off fluid.

Joe's face was somber. This was the first time he had ever been seriously injured playing any sport. One thing was for sure, Joe promised himself. From now on he would always wrap that white tape around his shoes. The first time he hadn't bothered, he'd been hurt. Joe wasn't superstitious, but he wasn't taking any chances.

Joe limped for the rest of the season. He played only occasionally, but Alabama rolled on unbeaten, winning four more big games. Late in November, the Tide prepared to meet Georgia Tech, the team that had ended their unbeaten string two years earlier. Still limping, Joe walked down the aisle at a pep rally, stepped onto the stage, and addressed an auditorium crammed with students.

"Two years ago we went to play Georgia Tech," Joe said, his voice now a soft drawl that he'd picked up in Alabama. "We had won eight straight and we were Number One in the country. We lost. This year we've won eight straight and we are Number Two in the country. Saturday we're going to win at Georgia Tech and we're going to come back the Number One team in the country!"

The students roared. Then they watched Joe hobble off the platform. They were sure he wouldn't be able to help 'Bama on Saturday, not the way he limped.

On Saturday, under a gray sky, the two teams struggled through a scoreless tie for much of the first half, Joe watching from the bench. With only a minute left in the half and the ball on the Tech 49, Bear Bryant turned to Joe and waved him into the game. The huge crowd stood when they saw number 12 limping onto the field in his all-white shoes.

In the huddle Joe called for a pass. It was batted down. Joe called for another pass. He threw. It bounced low at the foot of his receiver. Joe growled, angry at himself.

In the huddle he called for another pass. He told his receiver, Dave Ray, to curl at the line of scrimmage, as though he were cutting back toward Joe. "Then pivot and take off," Joe told Ray.

Joe stepped back into the pocket. He saw

Knee aching, Joe arches a long pass in 'Bama's second-half rally against Texas in the 1965 Orange Bowl.

Ray pivot, then burst away from his defender. Joe arched a long pass that Ray caught on the run at full speed on the 20 and carried to the one. From there fullback Steve Bowman blasted into the end zone and Alabama led, 7-0.

That spark ignited the 'Bama machine. It rolled over Georgia Tech, 24-7, to remain unbeaten and return to Tuscaloosa acclaimed the nation's Number One team.

For the third straight season, Alabama was invited to a bowl game — this year back to the Orange Bowl in Miami against Texas. A few days before the game, Joe was working out with his teammates. He cut, leaning hard on that right knee. The knee collapsed under him. Joe flopped to the grass, grasping the knee, the pain showing in the glitter of his eyes. He'd reinjured the knee. Doctors said he would not be able to play in the Orange Bowl. "I'll play," Joe said.

The evening of New Year's Day, a huge crowd filled the Orange Bowl. Number 12 trotted out with the Alabama team, white shoes glistening in the lights, and the crowd saw that Joe was limping noticeably. They saw him watching the game from the bench for most of the first half, busy urging his teammates to move against Texas. But it was Texas who moved, scoring two touchdowns to take a 14-0 lead.

Bear Bryant turned to Joe, as he had turned to him so often the past three years. Joe responded. In this, his last game for 'Bama, Joe jerked on his helmet and limped out onto the field.

Joe started to throw passes. He completed six and 'Bama had a touchdown, trailing now 14-7. Texas roared back with another touchdown to lead at the half, 21-7. In the early part of the second half, Joe zipped four passes into the hands of receivers, the last one a twenty-yard toss to Ray Perkins in the end zone: Texas 21, Alabama 14.

Alabama held Texas and now Joe had the ball again. He passed 'Bama into Texas territory. Alabama kicked a field goal: Texas 21, Alabama 17.

A determined Texas team staved off several more 'Bama challenges, and now there were only three minutes left to play. Texas dropped back to protect against the long Namath touchdown pass. Joe sent his backs scurrying through the strung-out defense for first downs. Alabama marched to the Texas six. Only a minute remained on the clock.

Three times Joe handed off to Alabama runners who slammed into the line. They reached the one-yard line. It was fourth down, with only one more chance to score.

In the huddle Joe called for a quarterback sneak. He would try to crash into the end zone, accepting all the pressure himself. The two teams lined up, near-exhausted after this head-to-head goal-line struggle.

Joe called the numbers. The huge crowd in the Orange Bowl was dead-quiet. Across the nation millions leaned forward tensely to watch their TV screens. Joe took the snap. He ploughed into the center of the line. He seemed to get a foot across the goal line. Then a half ton of Texas flesh and bone hurled him back. The whistles blew, and officials ruled Joe had not scored. It was only Joe's third defeat in his three years at 'Bama, each defeat as close to victory as a touchdown.

Joe walked slowly off the field, the big crowd standing and applauding him. 'Bama cheerleaders wept, saying good-bye to Joe Willie Whiteshoes. He was limping a little and one pro-football scout, watching him leave the stadium, said to another: "He's great, the best I've ever seen. But do you really think he is worth $400,000?"

He'd Make It—
One Way or the Other

THE ST. LOUIS CARDINAL football official was talking to a reporter. "There is no question that Namath is a great quarterback," he told the reporter. "We have offered him $389,000 to sign with us. But he wants to play in New York. We are not going to offer him a cent more. We are dropping out of the bidding at $389,000."

The New York Jets were bidding for Joe against the Cardinals of the NFL. The Jets of the new American Football League were owned by David (Sonny) Werblin. A veteran of show business, Sonny Werblin knew the value of a star. A star's name, shining in lights on a marquee, could line up people at the box office. Sonny Werblin thought that Joe could become a nationally famous star.

"He's exciting to watch when he steps back in those white shoes and tosses those long passes," Sonny told his friends. "He could bring people into the park to watch the Jets and the entire American Football League. He'd have people watching the American Football League games on television."

The Jets — and the AFL — desperately needed to attract people. And they badly needed money from the television networks for their games. In New York, for example, fans squeezed into Yankee Stadium to watch the NFL Giants. Rows of empty seats watched the Jets. Before one game a Jet player looked at the empty seats and said, "There are more players here than spectators." New York fans laughed at the Jets, who had lost more games than they'd won. And many sports fans scorned the new American Football League. "Minor league," the fans said. "It has no real stars."

"This Joe Namath can be great," Sonny Werblin told his business associates. "He can be as important as Red Grange was to the NFL when it got started. A star. Someone people will knock down gates to see. And he's always been a winner. He can make winners of the Jets."

To persuade Joe to sign with the Jets, Werblin offered him a little more than $400,000 for a three-year period. "You'll like New York," Sonny told Joe and his agent, Mike Bite, his old pal from Alabama. Joe agreed. He liked the rat-tat-tat, fast-paced life of New York, its Broadway shows, its excitement, its beautiful girls, its night life. Joe said yes, he'd sign with the Jets.

JETS SIGN $400,000 QUARTERBACK

That headline flashed across sports pages from coast to coast. Suddenly the Jets, and the AFL, were big league in the eyes of many fans. They had spent more money to sign a ballplayer than the NFL had ever spent. And Joe Namath was famous almost overnight as the $400,000 quarterback.

Some of Sonny Werblin's friends told him he was crazy. "How can you sign a quarterback with a bad knee for all that money?" they asked.

"We'll fix the bad knee," Werblin said.

A few weeks after Joe signed, he entered a

New York hospital. There Dr. James Nicholas cut into the knee and removed the torn cartilage.

Outside the operating room, Sonny Werblin paced anxiously. Suppose the operation wasn't a success? Joe could be the highest-priced football spectator in history. "You've thrown away $400,000," a friend told Sonny. "You'll have to pay Joe $400,000 for three years even if he doesn't play a game."

Dr. Nicholas came out of the operating room. He looked into Sonny's anxious face. "Everything went perfectly," Dr. Nicholas said. "The operation was a success." He added that Joe would have to wear a brace on the knee when he played. "But he'll be able to run fast enough to be a pro quarterback," Dr. Nicholas said.

Joe flew south to Alabama to continue his college education. Each day he draped thirty-pound weights onto his ankle and flexed the knee, strengthening it. At first, when he tried to run, the knee was stiff, as though there were a bowling ball inside it. But gradually Joe felt the stiffness melt away. He was dropping back to pass almost as quickly as he ever did. And he knew he could always zip a pass into a receiver's hands at the sideline.

That is the toughest pass for a quarterback, because it is so easily intercepted. He could throw passes to receivers while sitting in rocking chairs, Joe told people, laughing. He could too! His knee might be sore but his right arm was still strong.

All across the country football fans debated. How would Namath perform as a pro? Already, even before he had played his first pro game, he was the AFL's best known player. People were lining up to buy tickets to Jet games. But Joe knew, as everyone else did, that he would be the butt of cruel jokes if he failed.

A friend went to see Joe at the Alabama campus. Joe was living in a ramshackle house he humorously called Namath's Mansion. Living with him were Jimmy Walsh and Ray Abruzzese, a former Alabama player who was now a back with the Buffalo Bills. They were throwing darts at a board on a wall when the visitor entered. Joe said hello, flipped some darts, and invited him to join the game.

Joe won the game easily, tossing dart after dart into the bull's-eye on the wall. When the game was over, Joe flopped onto a chair and began to answer questions in his soft drawl.

The friend asked Joe about all the $400,000-quarterback publicity. "A lot of people expect you to be a great quarterback right from the start," the friend said. "Is this the biggest challenge of your life?"

Joe smiled. "Your next challenge is always the biggest challenge," he said. "Everything is a challenge. Studying in college was a challenge. Studying can be hard; I was homesick. But I stuck. The big thing is: You attack each challenge the same way, as if it were the biggest. That's the only way to do it."

He paused. "Look," he said, "it is true that I did feel some pressure at first with all this publicity. But then I got close to myself and I said, 'Put all your effort into this, be honest with yourself, do your best.' Then that's it. You can do no more than your best."

Again he paused. Then he said, "Take everything into account: my injury, all the publicity, all those things you've mentioned. And just throw them away. *Because I am going to make it.*" His voice rose, loud and clear. "Maybe I'll make it as a defensive back, maybe I'll make it as a quarterback, *but I am going to make it.*"

"You sound cocky," his friend said.

"Everyone is cocky to a certain degree,"

Joe said, unsmiling. "If you talk only about yourself, the cockiness has gone too far. I don't think that's happened to me. Or ever will. Anyway, confidence is a better word than cockiness. If you're a quarterback, always handling the ball, you've got to have confidence."

A few months later Joe seemed to exude confidence as he stepped out of a black limousine at the Jets' training camp in Peekskill, New York. He walked with a slight swagger as he carried his bags up to the room of the dormitory. Some of the Jet veterans stared at Joe, showing their dislike. Some veterans were receiving less than $20,000 a year while this kid, this rookie, was getting over $100,-000 a year. A little earlier one NFL veteran, Cleveland quarterback Frank Ryan, had said, "If Namath is worth $400,000, I'm worth a million." A lot of people agreed with him.

Now some of the Jet veterans were saying similar things. The loudest grumbler was linebacker Wahoo McDaniel. Wahoo had been the Jet star. Whenever Wahoo made a tackle, the Jet fans roared, "Wahoo... Wahoo..."

Now Wahoo realized that the eyes of the fans would be only on Joe. He didn't like that, nor did the other veterans. "I've been a pro football player for five years," one said. "What has this kid Namath ever done?"

At practice Wahoo hurled insults at Joe. Some of Wahoo's friends laughed when Joe overthrew a receiver. "What's a-matter, kid?" they yelled. "You too rich to throw a ball straight?"

"He can only see dollar signs," yelled someone else.

Joe ignored the taunts. The next time he stepped back to pass, he threw the ball directly into the hands of a receiver.

Just before the start of the season, the veterans called a team meeting in the locker room. One veteran stood up and said, "This is a meeting to get everyone together before we start the season. If anyone has any gripes, speak up now. Don't keep them hidden."

Several players got up and spoke, suggesting ways to unite the team. Then there was a long pause. The veterans glanced at Joe. They expected the high-priced quarterback, the team's leader, to speak.

Joe stood up. He told the players he knew that some of them resented all the money he was making. He knew they were angry that he was playing with a three-year contract so he could not be cut, as they could. But

Joe wanted the players to know something. He was there to win. That's all. To win. He wanted to help make the Jets winners as he had helped to make Alabama winners. One day the Jets could be the world champions of football. He was here to see that day come.

Joe stopped. The room was silent. A lot of people, he said, had been saying that Joe Namath didn't care whether the Jets won or lost.

Joe slowly looked around the room. Would anyone want to stand up right now and make that accusation?

No one stood. There was a long silence. Then Joe sat down.

Later, outside the clubhouse, a Jet player said, "Now I know what they mean when they say he is a star. There is something about him when he speaks. Everyone stops talking and listens."

"He's cool," said another player. "He doesn't seem to have a nerve in his body."

The Jets began the season with Mike Taliaferro, their quarterback of a season ago, as the number-one quarterback. Jet owner Sonney Werblin was angry. He wanted the coach, Weeb Ewbank, to start Namath.

"He's not ready," Ewbank told Werblin.

Namath looks for a receiver: "Your next challenge is always your biggest."

"When will he be ready?"

"It will take time. I've been watching Joe throw. He played part of last year with that bad knee and developed some bad habits. From favoring that bad knee he lost his footwork and started throwing just with his arm. He's got to overcome those bad habits."

The coach laughed, almost to himself. "All these young quarterbacks have to learn," he said. "They have such strong arms, they think they can throw a ball through a concrete wall. I coached Johnny Unitas when he was a rookie. He thought he could fire that ball through a crowd of defenders into a receiver's hands. Joe tries to do the same thing. No one can do that, not even a Unitas, not even a Namath. Joe will have to learn, as John did, that you have to needle those passes through the holes of the defense into the hands of the receivers."

Joe watched from the bench as Taliaferro called the signals for the Jets in their first game of the 1965 season. He did not get into the game as Houston beat the Jets, 27-21.

The next week Kansas City was beating the Jets. Ewbank sent in Joe midway through the second period. Joe completed 11 of 23 passes, but the Jets lost.

Joe started the third game — against Buffalo. He completed 19 of 40 passes. But the Jets lost.

Joe started against Denver. He completed 18 of 34 passes. But again the Jets lost.

Joe started the fifth game of the season, against Oakland. He completed only five passes in 21 tries and was hammered to the grass over and over again by a ferocious pass rush. The Jets lost.

Ewbank put the battered Joe back on the bench the next week against San Diego. He sent out Taliaferro to try to guide the Jets to their first victory of the season. The Chargers piled up a huge lead. With the game lost, Ewbank sent in Joe for the final five minutes.

In the huddle Joe called for a running play. As he walked out of the huddle toward the line, looking at the San Diego defense, something caught his eye, like a bright penny at the bottom of a pool.

The San Diego defense was expecting a run, and Joe knew it.

How could he tell? There was something Joe had seen, a change in the San Diego defense. A key, as the quarterbacks say. And that one key unlocked the door to the San

Diego defense. Joe could look into it and see what San Diego was planning to do.

Joe changed the play at the line, calling for a pass. He completed the pass. He completed another pass. He completed four of six passes in the closing minutes. The completions meant nothing, for the Chargers were easy 34-9 winners. But as he walked off the field Joe knew he no longer was wearing the blindfold of inexperience. Now he could look at a defense and see whether the defense was expecting a pass or a run.

Joe remembered what his friend, Charger quarterback John Hadl, had told him: "Know the keys. You're nothing if you don't know the keys. Know the keys and you're everything."

A lot of Jet fans didn't think Joe was anything at all. With the Jets losing their first six games, some fans were calling Joe a flop.

Weeb Ewbank knew differently. He had seen Joe operate like a skilled surgeon against that Charger defense. He started Joe in the Jets' seventh game. Joe coolly slashed apart the Denver Bronco defense with runs up the middle and to the flanks. He threw only six passes (and completed five), the Jets routing Denver, 45-10, for the team's first victory. The following week, however, Ewbank still didn't think Joe was ready to be a number-one quarterback in the pros. Against Kansas City, Weeb started Taliaferro.

"Throw short," Ewbank told Taliaferro before the game. Taliaferro nodded. The game began. Taliaferro stepped back into the pocket. He threw a long pass. He stepped back again and threw another long pass.

"Throw short, throw short!" Weeb was screaming from the sideline.

Joe, watching from the bench, looked at the Kansas City defense. He noticed how it was hanging back. There was plenty of room over the line of scrimmage for short passes, he realized. But Taliaferro kept throwing long.

"Get in there," Weeb snapped at Joe. "And throw short."

Joe trotted out onto the field. He threw short, dartlike passes, completing seven of 16, and the Jets beat the Chiefs, 16-7, in one of the season's biggest upsets.

After the game the team flew back to New York. On the plane Ewbank turned to the newspaper reporters seated behind him and he said, "Joe is now our number-one quarterback."

With Joe at the helm, the Jets won four of

their last seven games to finish in second place in the AFL Eastern Division with a 5-8-1 record, their best finish ever.

Near the end of the season the Jets were leading Boston, 27-20, with fourteen minutes to play in the game. The Jets had the ball on their 20.

Joe looked at the Boston defense. He saw it strung out, looking for one of his long passes to his lanky receiver, Don Maynard. Joe handed off to halfback Bill Mathis, who gained up the middle. With third down and one yard to go, Joe saw the Boston defense clogging the middle, expecting a fullback plunge. Joe handed off to Matt Snell, who slid off-tackle for the first down.

Mixing runs and passes, Joe confused the Boston defense. When he saw the defense falling back, he called for a run. When he saw it bunch up to stop the run, he called for a pass. He threw to George Sauer over the middle and George weaved through the spread-out defense for thirty-three yards to the Boston 34. From there Joe steered the Jets to the 17. There, on third down, Joe saw the Patriots were looking for a short screen pass to the outside. Joe handed off to fullback Matt Snell who bulled up the middle to the eight. From there the Jets kicked a field goal to lead, 30-20.

Joe, walking off the field, looked at the clock. Fewer than five minutes remained in the game. He smiled. He had used up nearly nine minutes. Now the Patriots had to hurry to get a touchdown. Quarterback Babe Parilli threw a pass which the Jets intercepted and the Jets were 30-20 winners.

Later Joe was telling someone how much that long march had meant to him. "I had known, since the San Diego game, that I could look at a defense and see what it was doing," he said. "But a lot of times, I didn't know what play to call against a defense. Now I can look at a defense and pick any of seven or eight plays – the one play that will get the most yards against that defense."

In the beginning of the season Joe had said, "I'll make the Jets." He had meant: "I'll make the Jets as a quarterback or as a defensive back or as something. But I'll make the team. Because that's what I want to be – a football player. I want to play football and I don't care what position I play."

Still, he had always hoped he would be a pro quarterback. Now — for the first time — Joe *knew* he was going to be a pro quarterback.

Is Joe Namath Quitting?

JOE TOOK THE SNAP from the center. He stepped back into the protective cup of blockers, watching skinny Don Maynard flying down the sideline. Joe cocked the ball in both hands, waiting to see if Don could burst ahead of the man covering him. Around Joe raged a fierce hand-to-hand battle between his blockers and the Houston pass rushers: hands were swinging, shoulder pads popping as giants collided, the crowd's roar was as loud as the ocean in a storm.

Joe ignored it all, face impassive. He saw Maynard veer far downfield, some fifty yards away and the size of a matchstick. Joe heard a lineman yell, "Look out, Joe . . . !"

Joe releases the ball: "Nobody," says an opponent, "gets rid of the ball faster."

Two big Houston linemen broke through the wall of Jet blockers. They dived at Joe. One speared Joe in the chest with his helmet. The other drove two big fists into Joe's abdomen.

Joe toppled backward. But his left hand grasped the shoulder pads of one of the tacklers, steadying himself for a split second. With a flick of his right wrist, like someone waving good-bye, Joe threw the ball as he fell backward, buried under the Houston tacklers.

Maynard, on the run, turned to see the ball drilling through the air, growing bigger and bigger as it arched fifty-five yards down the field. Don was ahead of his man by half a stride. He reached out, snared the ball with his bony fingers, then ran into the end zone for a touchdown.

The Jets won this 1966 game, 52-13, Joe throwing five TD passes. After the game, the two frustrated Houston linemen sat unhappily in a corner of the dressing room. "That Namath is amazing," one was saying. "You hit most quarterbacks that hard, you'd knock the ball right out of their hands. But Namath, he has that amazing quick release. Nobody gets rid of a ball faster. I think he could throw that ball sixty yards even when he was stretched out on the grass."

The AFL linemen were all talking about Joe's quick release and his passing accuracy. Meanwhile the Jets won their first three games of the 1966 season to lead the Eastern Division. But coach Weeb Ewbank, preparing for the fourth game, frowned when he saw Joe limping through practice.

"It's his left knee that hurts," Weeb was telling a reporter one day. "That's the so-called good knee. It was the right knee the doctors operated on. But Joe has injured the left knee by leaning on it too heavily. He favors the left knee over the right knee. Now that left knee is aching something awful. It's like a toothache."

The reporter saw Jet offensive captain Sam DeLuca, a huge offensive guard, walking across the practice field. He talked to DeLuca about Joe. "That left knee is paining Joe all during practice," DeLuca said. "They give him shots so it won't hurt him during the games. But it aches after the games all week long. I'll say this for Joe: Not once have I heard him complain about the pain. And he'll never use his injured knees as an excuse when he has a bad day."

Joe seemed to be having a bad day the following Sunday against Boston. The Patriots were leading, 24-7, going into the last period. Then Joe began to put the ball into the hands of his receivers. He lofted two touchdown passes into their hands and the Jets rallied for a 24-24 tie.

The San Diego Chargers came into Shea Stadium for the Jets' fifth game of the season. A crowd of 53,497 filled every seat. It was the first sellout crowd in Jet history, and the biggest crowd in the history of the AFL. In only a year Sonny Werblin had made his $400,000 quarterback pay off. The Jets were winning, playing before large crowds. Suddenly they were almost as popular in New York as the NFL Giants.

Before the game the Chargers told each other, "We got to stop Joe Willie. We stop Joe Willie's passes, we stop the Jets."

For most of three periods the Chargers did stop Joe Willie. San Diego led, 16-10, with only eight minutes left in the game. Joe saw that the Chargers were looking for him to pass. Joe called for runs by Emerson Boozer and his other backs, and the Jets stormed down the field. On the San Diego eight Joe called for a sweep by Boozer. The big back

75

sped toward the left side behind a screen of blockers, turned the corner, and wiggled into the end zone for a TD. The Jets were still unbeaten, 17-16 winners over the Chargers.

Exultant Jet fans crowed that the Jets were now New York's best football team. The Giants were on their way to a sorry 1-12 record. "Who said the Jets were minor league?" a Jet fan asked a Giant fan one evening, as they were on their way home in the subway.

"You were minor league," snapped the Giant fan, "until you got Joe Namath."

The war between the two leagues was ending. The NFL admitted now that the AFL was major league. The two leagues agreed to meet each other after the 1966 season in an annual Super Bowl game. "It was Joe Namath who ended the war between the leagues," one AFL executive declared. "His signing and his success proved to the NFL that the AFL was here to stay."

Jet fans sat up at night dreaming of seeing Joe Willie and the Jets beat an NFL team like the Packers in the Super Bowl. Then the bubble burst. The Jets lost a game. They lost again, their offense and defense weakened by injuries. But they finished third in the Eastern Division with a 6-6-2 record, the team's

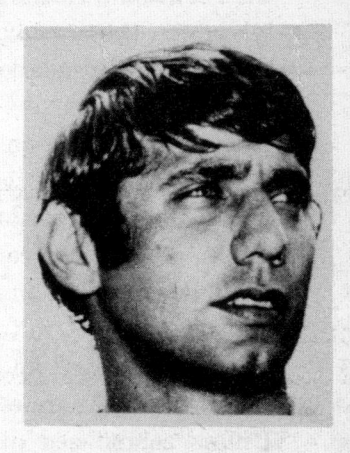

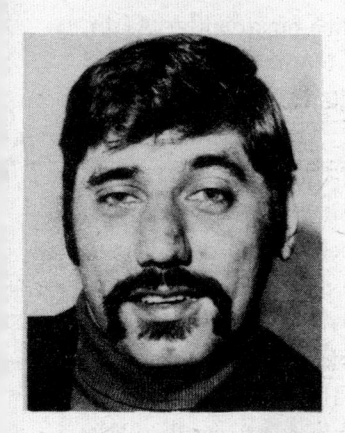

The various faces of Joe.

first nonlosing season since way back in 1960, when the AFL had started. And Joe was named the second quarterback on the All-Star AFL team.

Looking back on what Joe had accomplished in only two seasons, a writer in *Sport* Magazine declared: "When you add it all up, you have to conclude that no quarterback in this decade has come into pro football and risen so high so fast. Not John Hadl, nor Bart Starr, not Fran Tarkenton. Nobody. In the past fifteen years, in fact, only Johnny Unitas established himself faster as a pro quarterback. But not even Unitas became a superstar at the box office so quickly. After two years as a pro, Joe Namath, only twenty-four, is a name more famous than any, apart from Unitas and Bart Starr, in pro football today."

Before the start of the 1967 season, the surgeons operated on Joe's ailing right knee. A few months after the operation the heavy cast was removed. Joe ran the length of a football field and trotted to the sideline with a wide smile on his face. He looked like a boy savoring his favorite piece of candy. His right knee felt firm. And his left knee didn't hurt.

"I can run out there now," he said to a friend, grinning. "On the pass rush they're not going to find me standing there like a tree. I'm going to be able to scramble away from them."

When the Jets reported to their Peekskill, New York, camp, Joe kidded with the fans who came to watch him throw. He kidded the reporters with stories that were put-ons. "I'm going to throw more touchdown passes this season than Unitas, Starr, *and* Tarkenton combined," he told a young reporter one day.

"Gee, Joe, really?"

"Sure I am," Joe said, winking, and the reporter laughed.

Even Coach Ewbank did not escape Joe's good-natured kidding. During practice one afternoon Joe threw a pass against the Jet defense.

"No, Joe," yelled the squat Weeb. "Didn't you see that linebacker right where you threw?"

"What linebacker, Weeb?" Joe asked, looking puzzled. Joe waved his hands in front of Weeb's face. "Can't you see all right, Weeb?" he asked. "You're not going blind, are you?"

"Gee, Joe," said Weeb, looking sheepish and standing on his toes to look at the defense.

"I'm sure there was a linebacker there...."

And then Weeb saw Joe laughing and knew he'd been another victim of the Namath put-on.

To relieve the monotony of the two-a-day drills at summer camp, Joe liked to go as often as he could to the one movie house in downtown Peekskill. After the movie he usually jumped into a taxi or his Cadillac and drove to Dooley's, a place where the Jet players liked to gather.

Joe walked into Dooley's one evening with a friend. "Good movie, Joe?" the players yelled.

"It was OK," Joe said, as solemn as a judge. "I'd say it was among the top thirty-eight of the year. Not among the top thirty-seven of the year, but among the top thirty-eight." He laughed.

A few days later, as Joe was throwing to his receivers, he stepped back to throw, and pain shot through the left knee. He slumped to the grass, gripping the knee, the pain drilling at his nerve endings. The knee felt as though someone had kicked it hard. A doctor looked at the knee. "It's only tendonitis," the doctor said. "A tendon is swollen and it's being rubbed raw by bone. But the swelling will go down. Don't worry."

Joe did worry. He remembered an uncle of his who had collapsed one day, his spine suddenly coming apart. Maybe Joe's knees were like his uncle's spine. Maybe one day Joe would be a cripple.

Joe couldn't sleep. One night he got a phone call from Beaver Falls. His mother was calling. One of Joe's brothers was ill. Joe didn't know what to do. He couldn't leave camp and go home. Or could he? Joe wanted to have time to decide what to do.

Joe visited Weeb. Could he leave camp and go to New York that night to think about his problems? The coach said no. The Jets were playing their first preseason game in only a few days. He wanted Joe to rest.

Joe stomped angrily out of Weeb's office. He jumped into his car and drove off, tires squealing. In Manhattan, not far from his penthouse apartment, Joe met some friends. They went to one of Joe's favorite East Side places to eat, drink, and talk. The hours glided by, with Joe too troubled to go back to his apartment or to the Jet camp. Joe began to talk loudly, saying a lot of things he didn't really mean. One eavesdropper thought Joe said he was going to quit pro football.

The man called a reporter. The next morning the story was on the front pages. Joe had quit the Jet training camp. He was going to retire from football. Weeb Ewbank phoned Joe at his apartment. He asked Joe if the stories were true.

"No," Joe said.

"Come on up to camp," Weeb said.

Joe dressed quickly, not even taking the time to shave. He steered his big car north toward Peekskill. At camp the players stood around in small knots and discussed Joe's leaving. "There goes our chance for a championship," one said. "Without Joe we can't go all the way."

"Yeah," said another, "and only because Joe wants more money."

"Where did you hear that rumor?"

"I heard it," said the player.

Other false rumors were being heard among the Jets. "Joe doesn't want to stay in camp at night anymore, even though the rest of us have to," one player said. "He wants special privileges because he's the star."

Joe drove his car into the camp. He got out and started toward Ewbank's office. In a hallway he was intercepted by Sam DeLuca. "Joe," Sam said, "a lot of rumors are floating around. The players want to talk to you about them."

"Fine," Joe said. His face was matted with beard, his eyes half closed; he had not slept very much. He went with Sam DeLuca to a room where the players were gathered, seated in wooden chairs. One player told Joe about the rumors going around: that he had gone to New York for selfish reasons.

Joe apologized to the players for leaving camp. He told them he had some personal problems he had hoped to solve. He said the rumors were untrue; he wanted to be as much a part of this team as anyone else, a star or a third-stringer. He wanted the Jets to be champions.

"We believe you, Joe," Sam DeLuca said. The players sensed that he was grateful. Then the coaches came into the room, and the players explained some of their grievances to the coaches, who listened sympathetically. Hidden grudges, some of them directed against Joe and some against other players, were being brought out into the open where they could be discussed and then forgotten.

Sam DeLuca was watching Joe. Sam

sensed that Joe was amazed by this meeting and hadn't known that the team cared so much about what he did. He had left for one night and the entire club had been torn by fears that he was leaving them. For the first time, Joe was beginning to realize how important he was to the Jets.

Joe wasn't just one of twenty-two starters, no matter how much he wanted to be one of the boys. Joe Willie Whiteshoes was the head and heart of this team. So without him it would collapse — and Joe Namath knew it. And now he also knew what his real responsibility was to his teammates.

How To Be a Leader

JOE STROLLED across the patio, greeting his friends who were talking and laughing and having a good time. Joe looked trim in white slacks, a lemon-colored sports shirt, and white buckled shoes. Lanterns illuminated this outdoor garden party, and the light gleamed on Joe's tanned face. Walking with Joe was tall, slender Suzie Storm. The blonde rock 'n' roll singer was his date that night in Birmingham, Alabama, where the Jets had flown for an exhibition game.

Many of the Jet players had come to the party, held at the home of Mike Bite's brother. The Jets' Dave Herman, Gerry Philbin, and a dozen other players mingled with the party guests, talking about the coming 1967 AFL season.

Joe spied a New York feature writer chatting with some guests and walked up to him.

"Get out of here," Joe snarled, pushing the writer in the chest.

The guests stared, surprised. Joe turned to them. "This writer is from New York," Joe said in his soft drawl. "He's going to write a bad story about me and ruin my reputation."

The guests glared at the writer, and Joe turned to one of them. "I want you to do me a favor," Joe said. "If this writer does a bad article on me, I want you to shoot him dead."

The guest's jaw dropped. The writer began to laugh. Then Joe laughed, his put-on joke accomplished. All the guests were laughing. Joe smiled at Suzie Storm, and the two of them walked off to join another group.

A few evenings later, in Birmingham, Joe stood under the goal posts of a football field as each Jet's name was announced. When the public address announcer bellowed, "... and from the University of Alabama, number 12, Joe Namath ... ," the Alabama crowd of some 55,000 stood and roared, welcoming home their Joe Willie Whiteshoes.

That night Joe played only two quarters, tossing a touchdown pass against the Kansas City Chiefs, who won the preseason game. Afterward, the Jets flew back to New York and their camp in Peekskill.

"Joe is throwing better than ever," a Jet player remarked one day in the camp dining room.

"He's the best in the AFL or NFL right now."

"The only thing that gripes me about him," said a third player, "is that the coaches aren't as tough on him as they are on the rest of us. He's Sonny Werblin's star. The coaches don't want to get Sonny mad at them by being tough on the star."

"Aw, forget that stuff," said a Jet. "Joe's a good guy. The other day he lent his car to a player who had to go to New York. That left Joe without a car, but that's the way he is — a real generous guy."

"And a real funny guy too," said another player. They began to talk about what Joe had said a few nights earlier in Dooley's.

Joe had been talking about his visit to a small Texas town. He had been bitten by a scorpion while in the town, he said, and had come close to dying.

"Aw, a scorpion can't kill you," one player said.

"A *bumblebee* can kill you," Joe shouted in his other voice, the loud, assertive one that smothered all arguments. "Last year there were 18,000 deaths due to bumblebee bites. Look it up."

The other players laughed, knowing Joe was fooling. He fascinated them. Whenever Joe talked, the other players stopped talking to listen. "He's like a magnet," one player said of him. "He grabs your attention and holds it."

A week before the start of the 1967 season, the Jets broke camp at Peekskill. The players went to their homes in New York City and the suburbs. Joe lived in a penthouse apartment high above First Avenue on Manhattan's East Side. From its terrace he could look down on the East River and the soaring bridges. One afternoon Joe gathered together his dirty laundry, shoveled it into a pillowcase, and said to a friend, "Let me drop off this laundry, then let's go and have something to eat."

Joe slung the pillowcase full of laundry over his shoulder, and he and his friend rode the high-speed elevator twenty floors to the

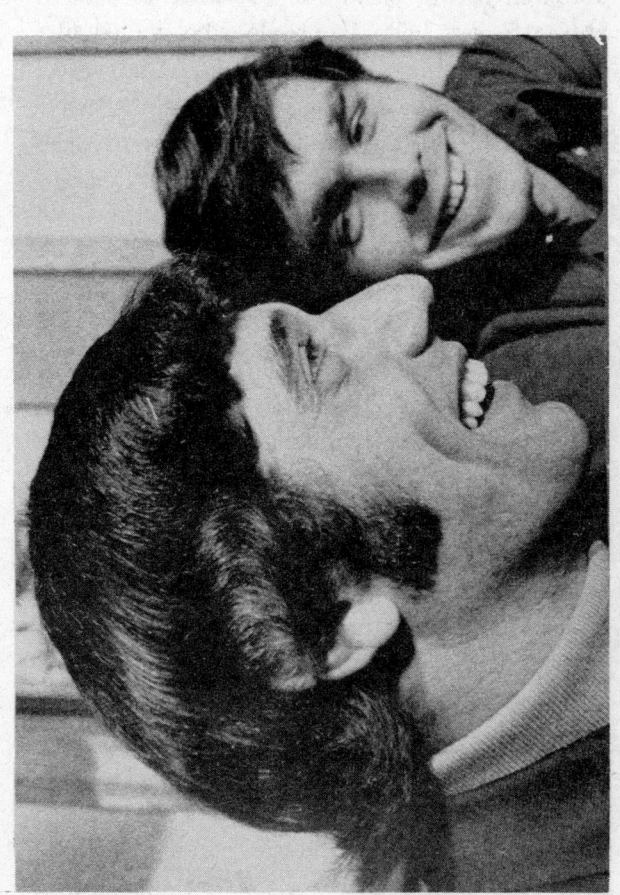

Joe Namath, with Derek Sanderson, smiles during a press conference.

street level. As they walked up First Avenue, a taxi driver honked his horn and waved at Joe. Joe waved back. Joe ducked into three stores to say hello to people who waved at him through the windows. At the laundry he handed the pillowcase bag to a girl clerk. She kidded him about the Jets' first game of the season, now only a few days away. "I hope you win," she said, "but I don't think you will."

Joe laughed. "The Jets will win," he said.

"I'm rooting for you," the girl said.

There are many plush, expensive restaurants on the East Side. But one of Joe's favorites is the Green Kitchen, a ham-and-eggs kind of place where Joe can sit on a stool along with truck drivers, schoolteachers, cabbies, plumbers, and errand boys.

Joe stepped into the Green Kitchen and hopped onto a stool. A smiling waitress handed him the menu. He ordered eggs and coffee. A waiter came by. Joe pointed a thumb at the empty stool next to him and invited the waiter to sit down. The waiter then began to tell Joe what was wrong with the Jets.

"You're not using enough screen passes, Joe," the waiter said. "Look, let me show you."

The waiter pulled a pad and a pencil from his pocket and drew a diagram of a screen pass.

Joe looked at the diagram. "That's a good play," Joe said, "when the linebackers are here."

Joe drew several circles in the diagram.

"But when the linebackers are here," Joe said, drawing another set of circles, "the screen pass won't get you very far."

"Hmmm," the waiter said, studying the circles.

The waiter left, and Joe turned to a friend who had asked him about being a leader in pro football. "It gets easier all the time, year by year, season by season," Joe said. "When you are a rookie quarterback, you can't tell a veteran what he is doing wrong. But after a veteran has watched you do things the right way for a season or two, he's a lot more willing to listen when you tell him what he's doing wrong. And when you are friendly with someone, it's easier to tell him what he is doing right and what he is doing wrong."

A good friend of Joe's came into the Green Kitchen and sat on the stool next to Joe. He overheard part of the conversation. "What a lot of people forget about Joe," he said, "is that he is a great student of the game. When Joe first joined the Jets, he took a test answering questions about the Jet plays. All the Jet players took the same test. Joe got the highest score. And he wasn't as familiar with the plays as the veterans were. You ask Joe a question about any Jet play and he can tell you where every man on the team is on each and every play."

Someone else asked Joe, "What quarterbacks do you admire as leaders?"

"There are three quarterbacks I admire a lot," Joe said. "I wouldn't try to rank them in any order. But I would name Johnny Unitas. I mention him because he is from Pennsylvania like myself." Joe laughed. "No, seriously," he said, "I've admired Unitas for a long time. He's a winner. And Bart Starr is also a winner."

Joe sipped his coffee. "And I'd also name Sonny Jurgensen. He has never been a winner at Washington. But you put Jurgy at Green Bay or Baltimore, and he would win. You put Starr or Unitas at Washington and what would happen?"

"They wouldn't win," said Joe's friend.

Joe nodded, his meaning clear: A quarterback must have the runners and the blocking if his team is to win. A quarterback can't turn a team into a winner all by himself.

At the start of the 1967 season, the Jets seemed to have the runners, the blocking, and the passing to win. In the first game of the season, however, burly fullback Matt Snell was smacked down hard by a tackler and limped off the field, his knee injured. Doctors said Snell wouldn't be able to play again until the middle of the season.

But the Jets could win without Snell. They scored on Joe's passes and the ground-gaining of young halfback Emerson Boozer. And the Jet defense was batting down passes and slamming down runners, yielding only one or two touchdowns in most games. Near the end of the season with only four games remaining, the Jets led the AFL's Eastern Division with a 7-2-1 record. If the Jets finished first in the Eastern Division, they would face the winner of the Western Division for the right to go to the Super Bowl.

But Boozer injured a knee and was lost for the season. Matt Snell came back but he wasn't running with his old slam-bang power. In a game against the Denver Broncos, Joe knew he would have to throw a lot of passes to score. Trouble was, the Broncos also knew that he would have to pass.

On play after play, Bronco linebackers blitzed in on Joe. They blocked his view of the receivers, chased him out of the pocket, and forced him to throw hurriedly. Joe threw sixty passes that day, twice what he normally threw, and six were intercepted. The Broncos won, 33-24.

The Jets lost their next game. Joe knew what the trouble was. He had no big back to keep the defenses "honest," as the quarterbacks say. "If I had a big back," he was saying one day, "I could give him the ball and send him through the line. The linebackers would have to worry about that big back running by them. They couldn't be blitzing all the time. And when I did pass, I could fake giving the ball to the big back. That would 'freeze' the linebackers a second or two and I'd have the time to set up and look for receivers."

The following week the Oakland Raiders were beating the Jets. Oakland's big pass rushers, led by six-foot-eight, 280-pound Ben Davidson, stormed in on Joe time after time. Davidson was as tall as a basketball center and as powerful as a circus strong man. On one play Joe faded back and saw Davidson bearing down on him. As Joe threw the ball, Davidson cracked into him, one of his fists whacking Joe across the side of the face.

Joe's helmet flew off. He reeled backward and dropped onto the grass. Joe rose slowly on one knee, his right hand holding the side of his face. Blood trickled along the side of his mouth. Joe shook his head, trying to shake away the fog that numbed his brain. He stood up and slowly walked back to the Jet huddle.

A few plays later he stepped back to pass. In charged Davidson. Joe threw high over Davidson's outstretched hands and arched the ball some forty yards for a TD. A little later he threw another touchdown pass. But the Jet defense crumbled before the Raider onslaughts, and the Raiders won, 38-29.

In the clubhouse after the game a doctor looked at Joe's swollen face. "The cheekbone is fractured," he told Joe.

"Well, fix it up, doctor," Joe said. "A couple of the guys and myself, we're planning to go to Las Vegas tomorrow on our day off. I don't want to miss any of the fun."

His face bandaged, Joe flew from Oakland to Las Vegas for some relaxation before he reported to the Jets in San Diego, where they were preparing for their last game of the season. If the Jets could beat the Chargers and if Miami could beat Houston on this last weekend, then the Jets would be the Eastern Division champions.

"Can you play, Joe?" a Jet coach asked a few days before the San Diego game.

Joe looked at the coach. Joe's face was so puffed it looked as if a bag of marbles were inside his cheek. "I'll play," he mumbled through swollen lips.

Two days later Joe trotted onto the field to play the Chargers, his cracked cheekbone protected by a special mask. Joe knew what he had to do: throw a lot of passes. "We don't have the running backs," Weeb Ewbank told Joe, "and we know that San Diego will score a lot against our defense. We have got to score faster than they do."

Joe threw twenty-six passes. He completed eighteen. Four of them were good for touchdowns. And the Jets walked off the field the 42-31 winners.

The Jets flew back to New York. Each man was rooting for Miami in its game the next day against Houston. Four of the Jets came up to Joe's apartment to watch the Miami-

Houston game on color TV. They cheered every good play by Miami; they were silent on every good play by Houston. When the game ended, there was silence in the room: Houston had won. Houston was the AFL Eastern champion.

"Look," someone finally said, "it wasn't that bad a season. We had our best record ever — eight wins, five losses, only one tie. We finished second in the East despite injuries to our two big backs. Next year, if everyone stays healthy, we can take the Eastern title."

The players quietly said their goodbyes and left Joe's place. He thought about the season. It had been a good year for him. He had gained 4,007 yards with his passes, becoming the first quarterback in history to gain more than 4,000 yards passing in one season. He led the AFL in completed passes for the 1967 season. And he ranked second in touchdown passes with twenty-six.

But Joe wasn't happy. There had been something missing from the season. Joe knew what it was — the Super Bowl.

A few days later a few of his friends were sitting around the apartment. That night Joe and his friends were going to a night spot to listen to The Supremes, a singing group that was one of Joe's favorites. Joe was mixing cold drinks for everybody at the bar against one wall of the long living room. Some of his friends were seated on a curving couch, talking or watching television. Others were standing on the terrace and watching the multicolored lights of Manhattan blink below them.

Mike Bite, Joe's old friend from Alabama and now his lawyer, relaxed on the couch. Mike stared at the thick white llama rug that covered the floor of the living room. "It would have been cheaper," Mike was saying to somebody, "if we had covered this floor with dollar bills."

Joe overheard. He laughed, tinkling the ice in an empty glass. A friend asked if he were looking forward to next season.

Joe nodded, smiling. Then a serious expression crossed his face. "I know what I'm looking forward to," he said, "I'm looking forward to seeing a Super Bowl game."

"You can get tickets to a Super Bowl game," a friend said.

"I don't want to buy my way in," Joe said. "I want to go in through the players' entrance."

"On to the Super Bowl...."

JOE TRUDGED SLOWLY off the practice field at Hofstra College on Long Island on this summer day in 1968. The Jets had moved their training camp from Peekskill to Hofstra. Joe wiped beads of sweat off his grimy chin. His green jersey stuck to his body in the hundred-degree heat. He walked up the wooden steps and into the cool Jet clubhouse. Cold drinks and trays of sliced meat had been placed on a table. Joe poured out a drink and gulped it down.

"How's the knee?" a player asked Joe.

"Feels all right," Joe said. "Today I felt real strong out there."

Several months earlier the team physician, Dr. James Nicholas, had operated on Joe's left knee, tightening tendons. Joe walked over to the table of food, served himself some meat, then flopped down wearily on a stool.

Through a window he could see the highrise campus dormitories. He and linebacker Jimmy Hudson were sharing a room on the tenth floor in one of those dorms. Joe saw Hudson on the other side of the clubhouse.

"Hey, roomie," Joe yelled. "Have you got our key?"

"You forgot it again," Hudson shouted back. "Here he is, our quarterback. He is supposed to remember all our plays. And he can't even remember his room key."

Joe smiled. He saw a sportswriter, Dick Young of the New York *Daily News*, coming toward him. Joe said hello. Young sat near Joe. "You heard some booing last season when you missed a receiver," Young said. "Does the booing by fans bother you?"

"I get angry occasionally," Joe said, "but not during a game. I don't listen to what the fans are yelling during a game. And when I do get angry about booing, well, you stop to consider how much they know about the game, you figure it's their ignorance showing.

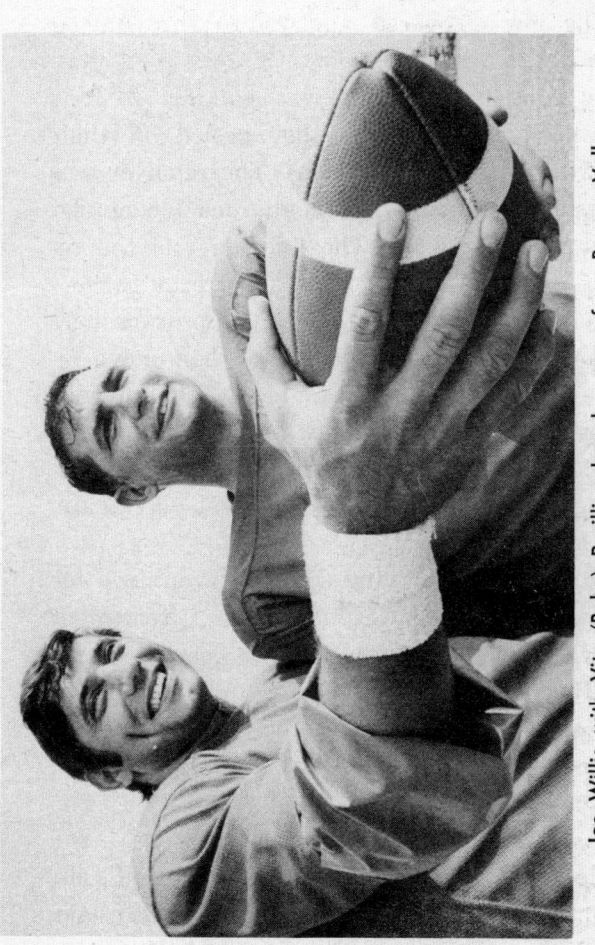

Joe Willie with Vito (Babe) Parilli, who also came from Beaver Valley, during a practice session at Hofstra campus in 1968.

You throw a ball fifteen yards over a guy's head. They think it's a bad pass. It could be the guy's covered and you're throwing it away to avoid a loss."

Another reporter was talking to Joe's offensive linemen as they peeled off their sweaty practice uniforms. The reporter was asking each man how he guarded Joe against the pass rushers. The linemen told the reporter how they blocked some pass rushers high and how they hit bigger pass rushers low across the knees to knock them down.

"Suppose you missed a block," the reporter said to center John Schmitt. "And suppose the man you missed were to tackle Joe, damaging Joe's knees so he could not play again. How would you feel?"

"We've been living with this ever since Joe came to the Jets," Schmitt said. "I remember when Joe joined the team, a coach told us: 'If your man gets to Joe and hurts those $400,000 knees, don't bother to walk back to the huddle. Just keep walking right out of the park!'"

Guard Randy Rasmussen overheard. "You feel terrible when Joe gets hit because it's our number-one job to protect him," Randy said. "You see him lying there after he has been hit, trying to catch his breath, and you can't say, 'Sorry, Joe.' I'll tell you: When he gets hit hard, even just once in a game, it ruins the game for me, even if we've won."

"I'll tell you what it feels like when the guy you're supposed to block hits Joe," said tackle Winston Hill, a 300-pound mountain of muscle. "It's like if someone were to walk up to your mother and punch her right in the face."

"Do you feel that way," asked the reporter, "because it's your job to protect Joe?"

"That's part of the reason," Winston said, "but it's not the only reason. I like Joe. He's a good, friendly guy by nature. He just gets along with everybody. There won't be another one like Joe Namath. Not with his talent and his individualism. Not in this century."

A few weeks later the Jets left Hofstra to open their 1968 season against the Kansas City Chiefs, always one of the best AFL teams. Early in the game, with the ball on the New York 43, Joe decided to surprise the Chiefs. The Chiefs were looking for a short pass to the sideline. Joe told his lanky receiver, Don Maynard, to fake toward the sideline, then wheel and race straight downfield on what the pros call a "bomb" or "fly" pattern.

Joe called the signals. Listening to the signals, Joe's two backs — Emerson Boozer and Matt Snell — knew they were to stick close to Joe to protect him against the pass rush. Joe needed time, all the time he could get, while Maynard raced fifty yards downfield.

Joe took the ball on the snap from center John Schmitt. He stepped back behind his wall of blockers. He looked to his left — away from Maynard's side. *One second ... two seconds* ... Joe would have three, maybe four seconds to release the ball before he'd be flattened by the pass rushers.

Now Joe swiveled his head and looked for Maynard. He saw him galloping down the sideline, a half step ahead of a Kansas City pursuer. Joe cocked his wrist and spiraled the ball on a low arc — what the players call "a clothesline." Don never slowed down, reaching out and snaring the ball, then running into the end zone for a 6-0 New York lead. That early lead helped the Jets edge the Chiefs, 21-20.

The Jets next beat Boston, then went north to take on a team that had always been tough for them: the Buffalo Bills. Since Joe had joined the Jets, the Bills had beaten the Jets four out of six times.

The Bills seemed certain to win again when they leaped into an early 17-7 lead. But the Jets did not quit, scoring twice to lead at the half, 21-20. Early in the third period Buffalo kicked a field goal to regain the lead, 23-21.

Joe began to flip pass after pass and the Jets marched toward the Buffalo goal line. He told George Sauer to cut toward the sideline for a pass. Joe threw to Sauer. A quick Buffalo defensive back, Butch Byrd, cut in front of Sauer and pulled down the pass. There was nothing in front of Byrd except daylight. He ran down the sideline with the interception for a touchdown.

A few minutes later Joe decided to toss another one of those dangerous sideline passes to Sauer. This time another Bill player, Booker Edgerson, jumped in front of Sauer, took the ball, and ran all the way for another TD. The Bills led, 37-21.

Joe was having a bad day. He knew it. A lot of quarterbacks, having a bad day, would stop throwing those dangerous sideline passes to their wide receivers. They would lob short flare passes to their backs, the kind of passes that are almost impossible to intercept.

Joe went right on throwing to his wide receivers. He hit two of them for touchdowns, and the Jets edged to within two points of the Bills, 37-35. But the Bills hung onto the ball to pin the first defeat of the season on the Jets.

Joe had thrown four touchdown passes to Jet players and three touchdown passes to Bill players. "No one else could do that except Joe," a reporter said after the game.

A few days later defensive end Gerry Philbin stopped Joe during practice. "Joe," Gerry said in a slow, patient voice, like a teacher talking to a pupil, "see this green jersey?" Gerry tugged at his green Jet jersey.

"This is a Jet jersey," Gerry said. "The Jets wear green. Throw to the *green* jerseys. Not to the white jerseys. To the *green* jerseys."

The Jet players laughed and Joe grinned. Later, in his autobiography, *I Can't Wait Until Tomorrow*, Joe wrote:

"We really came together in 1968 — no cliques, no friction, no resentment.... Most of us were under thirty and we kind of represented the younger generation. We were into what's happening today in clothes, in music, all that sort of stuff. We went through training camp listening to the Fifth Dimension singing "Stone Soul Picnic" and we went through the season listening to Glen Campbell singing "Wichita Lineman." ... When I think of the 1968 season I still think of those two songs before I think of anything else...."

Halfway through the season the Jets lost to Denver. But they held first place in the Eastern Division by a slender margin. During practice one day, big defensive lineman Verlon Biggs suggested that all the players stop shaving until the team won the Eastern championship. "It will be a sign of our team unity," Biggs said.

"Good idea," Joe yelled. Joe began to grow a small beard and a mustache. He let his hair grow long. The Jets won their next game. Within a few weeks nearly all the Jets had beards or mustaches and long hair.

Some fans wrote to the club, protesting that long hair looked terrible on football players. The president of the AFL wrote to Joe and asked him to shave off his beard and cut his hair. The AFL president complained that Joe didn't look like a football hero in a beard.

He thought that Joe looked too much like a hippie.

Joe refused to shave off the beard. "I don't think there is anything wrong with beards and long hair," Joe told a friend. "The greatest man in the history of the world had long hair and a beard. He wasn't a hippie, was he?"

Joe's beard grew fuller. And the Jets rolled to victory after victory. They beat the Chargers; they beat the Dolphins. They faced the Cincinnati Bengals, needing only one more victory to clinch the Eastern championship. They beat the Bengals and were champions of the East.

After that victory an advertising executive spoke to Joe. Would Joe clip off his beard with a certain brand of electric razor? And would he clip off the beard in front of TV cameras? If Joe would say yes, the ad man would give him a check for $10,000.

Joe said he would be happy to accept the $10,000. TV viewers across the country watched Joe shave off the beard in a commercial for the electric razor.

"Imagine getting $10,000 for shaving," a Jet yelled in the clubhouse one day.

"I still have my mustache," said end Bake

Turner. "I'll shave it off right now. Give me a bid. What do I hear?"

"Will you take a quarter?" one Jet player sang out. All the Jets laughed. None was jealous of Joe. None envied him for making the $10,000. Joe had turned the Jets into winners. And winners get bigger paychecks. Winners go to the Super Bowl where the prize is $15,000 a man.

The Jets were only one game away from the Super Bowl. To enter the Super Bowl the Jets first would have to defeat the Oakland Raiders, the champions of the AFL's Western Division.

Joe didn't like the Raiders. He remembered how Ben Davidson had fractured his cheekbone in that game with the Raiders a year earlier. Joe thought that some of the Raider players were, as he said, "cheap-shot artists." In pro football a cheap-shot artist is someone who hits another player after he's been knocked down.

Oakland's towering Ben Davidson twirled his mustache and grinned when he heard what Joe had said. Ben thought he had hit Joe cleanly. "He gets paid enough to get hit, doesn't he?" Davidson growled. "On Sunday we'll hit him again hard enough to let him know he's earning his money."

Some 62,000 fans poured into New York's Shea Stadium on a bleak, wintry December day to watch the Jets battle the Raiders for the AFL championship. At first the Jets seemed stronger, pushing to the Oakland 14. From there Joe snapped a short pass to Don Maynard who scooted into the end zone for a touchdown. A little later Jim Turner kicked a field goal and the Jets led, 10-0.

Oakland rallied. The Raiders' tall quarterback, Daryle Lamonica, tossed short passes to rangy end Fred Biletnikoff and long passes to the fleet Warren Wells. Oakland scored a TD. Early in the third period Oakland veteran George Blanda kicked a field goal to tie the game, 13-13.

After the kickoff Joe dispatched his two backs, Matt Snell and Emerson Boozer, through holes in the Oakland line. The Jets smashed to the Oakland 20. Joe, back to pass, saw his tight end, Pete Lammons, cutting across the middle of the field, two Oakland backs sandwiching Pete between them.

Joe pegged the pass between the two defenders. Pete caught the ball and squirmed into the end zone. The Jets led, 20-13.

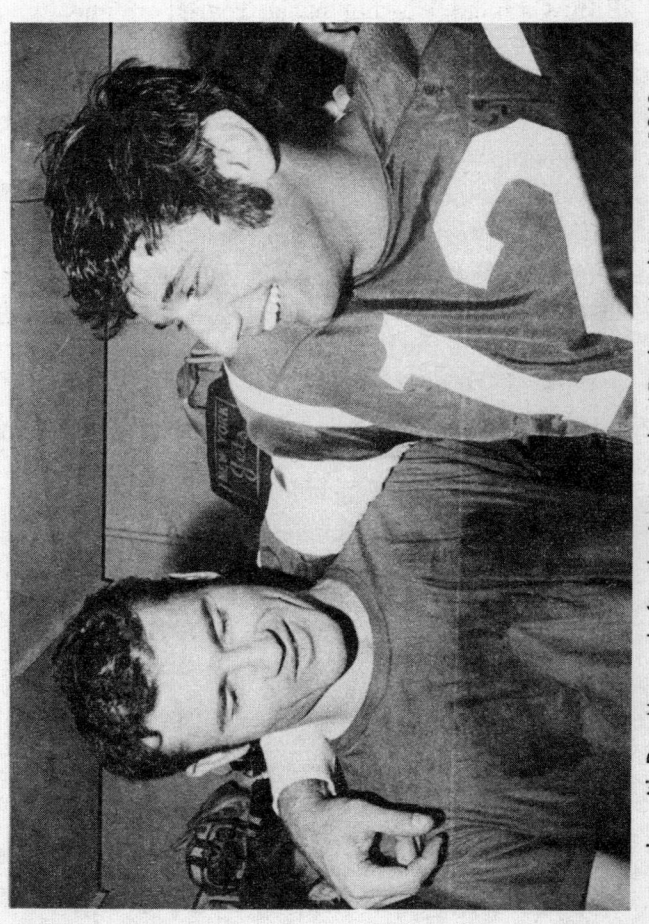

Joe with Don Maynard after the Jets won the AFL championship game in 1968.

Now Oakland came back. Lamonica lofted a pass to Biletnikoff. He threw to tight end Billy Cannon. His big backs roared up the middle. The Raiders stormed to the Jet 20. But there the Jet defense held. George Blanda came in and kicked a field goal. The Jets still led, 20-16.

A raw wind was whipping off Flushing Bay and into Shea Stadium, reddening the fingers of Daryle Lamonica as he cupped his hands under his center. Lamonica took the snap, gripping the ball in his frigid hands. He handed off to his backs who ploughed ahead for gains of five yards . . . ten yards . . . fifteen yards. Between plays Lamonica clapped his hands to warm them. From the Jet four he handed off to Pete Banaszak who bounded through the Jet line and dived into the end zone for a TD. The Raiders led, 23-20, with only a few minutes remaining.

Joe trotted out onto the field in his white shoes, warming his hands under his armpits. The Jet fans began a rising roar, beseeching Joe for one more touchdown and a Jet victory.

In the huddle Joe called for a pass. He scooted backward, turned, and saw George Sauer open. Joe threw the ball high to Sauer who leaped, caught it, and toppled to the grass on the Jet 42.

Joe studied the defense, then leaned into the Jet huddle. The ball was a long fifty-eight yards from victory and time was ticking away. Joe called for the long "bomb" to Don Maynard.

Joe took the snap and hurried eight yards back into his cup of blockers, "setting up," as the passers say. He threw. The ball soared some fifty yards in the air. The Oakland back, covering Maynard, leaped for it. The ball arched inches over his fingers and dropped into Maynard's straining hands. The Oakland back, coming down to the turf, bounced off the grass like a rubber ball and knocked Maynard down.

Don jumped up and looked at the sideline marker. The ball was on the Oakland six-yard line.

The roaring of Jet fans swelled over Shea Stadium, now lit by artificial lights in the wintry evening dusk. The Jets needed only six yards for victory and a trip to the Super Bowl.

Joe and the Jets knew how tough the going would be for those six yards. The big Oakland defense dug in, ready to hurl back the Jet runners. And now the Oakland pass defenders could play belt-buckle tight to the Jet pass catchers. They didn't have to worry about Jet pass catchers' getting ahead of them. The Jet pass catchers could run to the rear line of the end zone and no deeper.

Joe figured the Raiders would put two men on each of his elusive wide receivers. He decided on a pass to Billy Mathis, one of his backs. "Nine option," Joe said in the huddle. The Jets clapped hands and swung out of the huddle.

The teams lined up, the players' breaths ballooning white into the frosty dusk. Joe barked out the signals, a hush spreading over the stadium. He took the ball in his frigid fingers. He looked for Mathis. Mathis was covered.

Joe turned and looked for George Sauer. Covered. He looked over the middle for tight end Pete Lammons. He couldn't see Lammons in the swirl of green-and-white jerseys. Two big Oakland linemen charged at Joe.

Joe looked toward the opposite side of the field. He saw Don Maynard in the corner of the end zone. Like a baseball shortstop throwing to first base, Joe pegged the ball low and hard all the way across the field. Maynard dived for the low throw, his cupped hands grazing the grass. He grabbed the ball, tumbled over, then leaped high into the air.

Touchdown! A tremendous shout rose skyward out of Shea Stadium. The Jets had won, 27-23. The Jets were AFL champions.

Joe ran off the field, his hands held high and forming a "V for Victory" sign. Inside the Jet clubhouse the players shouted, yelled, and embraced each other. Once the patsies of the league, the Jets were now league champions. The players knew who had guided them to that championship. "Joe," they yelled, "beautiful, Joe, you were beautiful...."

Joe grinned. He pointed to his white pants, stained by grass and turf after he'd been knocked down by an Oakland pass rusher. "Hey, Talamini," Joe yelled to one of his linemen, Bob Talamini, "look at these pants. I don't want to get these pants this dirty in our next game."

"When's our next game?" someone shouted, grinning.

"On to the Super Bowl!" Joe yelled. "On to the Super Bowl!"

Joe Guarantees It

THE JET AIRLINER bumped down gently at Fort Lauderdale airport; sped along down the runway; then turned, slowed, and stopped. A yellow bus chugged toward the plane as the whine of the jet engines faded. The door of the airliner swung open and out came the New York Jets, arriving in Florida for the Super Bowl game against the Baltimore Colts.

Joe was right behind his pal, linebacker Jim Hudson. Photographers rushed up to Joe, flashing light bulbs in his face. "How will you do against the Colts, Joe?" a reporter shouted.

"We'll win," Joe shouted back, grinning.

"The Colts are favored by eighteen points," the reporter reminded Joe.

"We'll win," Joe repeated.

He and the other Jets climbed into the bus. The bus drove the team to a motel in Fort Lauderdale. Here the Jets would stay during the next week as they practiced for the Colts. Joe and Jim Hudson roomed together. For the first few evenings, Joe stayed in the room and stared at movies of the Baltimore defense. One evening Jim said to Joe, "Let's go out and relax," and Joe agreed.

They went to a restaurant in Fort Lauderdale. Joe and Jim were talking with friends when a broad-shouldered, bull-chested man walked up to Joe. "Hiya, Joe," the big man said. Joe turned. "Hiya, Lou," Joe said, shaking hands with Lou Michaels, the veteran place kicker and tackle for the Colts. Joe and Lou were old friends.

"Joe," Lou said, "we're gonna kill you."

Joe laughed. "You don't have a chance, man," he said.

"We'll beat you by thirty points," Lou said.

Again Joe laughed. "You really got to be crazy," he said. "You're not even gonna win the game."

Confident, competent Joe in action...

"I'll tell you why we're gonna win," Lou said. "I'll tell you why we're so confident. We got the man..."

"You mean Johnny?"

Johnny was Johnny Unitas, number 19, Joe's high school idol. Joe knew that Johnny's arm was aching.

"Well, I agree he's been great," Joe said. "But he can't throw across the street..."

"You wait and see what happens," Lou snapped.

"Yeah, I'll wait and see, man," Joe said, laughing.

Joe's laughter infuriated Michaels. He clenched his fists and talked about fighting Joe right there.

Joe threw up his hands, grinning, and said he wasn't going to fight any 240-pound tackle. Joe stood six-foot-two and weighed 200 pounds, big enough, but he wasn't the size of Lou. Anyway, he liked Lou. He told Lou he'd do his fighting on the football field.

The next day Joe went back to staring at the movies of the Baltimore defense. He was sitting with one of his receivers, tight end Pete Lammons. "I love what that one-eyed monster, that movie projector, is showing me," Joe said.

Pete nodded. "They don't look that tough," he said.

"I just hope they blitz against us," Joe said. He watched the screen as the Colt linebackers blitzed Los Angeles passer Roman Gabriel. The blitzers buried Gabriel.

"Let 'em blitz," Joe said to Lammons. Joe knew he had the big backs like Matt Snell who could knock down the blitzers. And Joe was sure he and his receivers could outwit the blitzers. He had seen his team in action when other teams lined up to blitz. Jet receivers would signal to Joe. Then they would dart into areas left vacant by the blitzers. When Don Maynard saw a blitz coming, he would wink at Joe. When Joe saw the wink, he'd know that Don would run an "I" pattern against the blitz. That "I" pattern usually left Don standing alone, ready for Joe's pass.

The movie ended. Joe flicked on the lights. He smiled at Lammons. "Pray that the Colts blitz," Joe said.

On the Thursday night before the game, Joe was invited to speak at the Miami Touchdown Club's annual dinner. At the dinner Joe received a trophy for being pro football's player of the year.

As Joe accepted the trophy, people stood up

and applauded. Joe looked at the dinner guests. In one hand he held the trophy, grasping the microphone with the other hand. Speaking softly and slowly, he said: "We're going to win on Sunday, I'll *guarantee* you."

The next day's newspapers flashed big headlines:

NAMATH "GUARANTEES" JET VICTORY

The Colt players growled and looked menacing when they read what Joe had said. Veteran lineman Billy Ray Smith crunched up the newspaper. "That Namath!" he snapped. "We're going to teach him humility on Sunday."

Some Jets were worried. "Hey," said one, "Joe's getting the Colts steamed up. They'll want to blow us off the field on Sunday."

"If they need Joe to get psyched up for a game as big as the Super Bowl," said another Jet, "they're in trouble."

"Right," said another player. "Joe is just trying to make us believe we're as good as the Colts or any other NFL team."

In the first Super Bowl game, the NFL's Green Bay Packers had demolished the AFL's Kansas City Chiefs, 35-10. In Super

Bowl 2, those same Packers had routed the AFL's Oakland Raiders, 33-14.

"Those AFL teams didn't believe they were as good as the NFL Packers," a Jet player said. "When they fell behind, they got panicky, and that cost them more touchdowns."

"That's right," said Gerry Philbin, the defensive end. "Joe doesn't want that to happen to us. The newspapers have been saying the Colts are the greatest team ever. Joe wants us to believe the Jets are the greatest team ever. Then, if we're behind by a touchdown, we won't panic or give up."

"Maybe," said a Jet player doubtfully, still looking at the headline. "But Joe is sure going to look foolish if we get whipped."

"I think Joe is deliberately putting this pressure on himself," said linebacker Ralph Baker. "Joe is at his best when the pressure is on."

While that conversation was going on, somewhere in Miami a familiar-looking man was staring at the newspaper headline through steel-rimmed spectacles. He put down the newspaper, smiling slightly, and noticed a newspaper columnist he knew. The columnist walked over and shook his hand.

"Hello, Vince," said the columnist.

Vince Lombardi, famous coach of the Green Bay Packers, was in Miami as a spectator. This year his powerful Packers had failed to make Super Bowl 3. They'd been beaten out by the Colts.

"Vince, will the Colts win easily?" asked the columnist.

"You know where my heart is," Vince said. His heart, of course, was with the NFL and its champions — the Colts.

"But do you think the Jets have a chance?"

"The Jets are capable of giving the Colts a good fight."

"You mean Namath."

"He's very dangerous and he has receivers who can catch the ball."

"How dangerous?"

"I better be going," Lombardi said, edging away. He didn't want to be quoted as saying the AFL had a chance to beat the NFL.

The columnist watched Lombardi go and remembered what Lombardi had said a few months earlier: "Namath's arm, his release of the ball are just perfect. Namath is as good a passer as I've ever seen. From what I've seen on the films, he's a perfect passer."

The columnist mused: Maybe the Jets did have a chance.

John Namath, Joe's father, had flown down from Beaver Falls for the game. He believed the Jets had more than a chance. He was telling everyone that the Jets would be champions. Two days before the game he walked into the Jet clubhouse. "Hello there, champ," he said to one Jet. "I'm going to call you all champs."

"Not yet. We haven't beaten them yet."

"You're going to win. You're the champions of all pro football."

The player laughed. "You're Joe's dad, all right," he said, "because Joe's been telling us that all week."

The next evening Joe was talking to his older brother, Bob, at the side of the motel pool. Joe and his brother were talking about Beaver Falls. "Remember when I took you to the movies on Saturdays when you were nine or ten?" Bob asked.

Joe smiled and nodded. Bob had been a good football player in Beaver Falls. Joe remembered how Bob had taught him how to throw a football.

They were silent a few moments, both staring at the leaden sky over Fort Lauderdale. Night was slowly descending on the eve of the big game. Suddenly Bob turned to Joe and said, "I didn't fly down here for nothing. Show me a winner."

Joe didn't say anything but he grinned.

Rain began to pelt Fort Lauderdale. Pass receiver Bake Turner watched the heavy drops spatter the sidewalk outside the motel. "We don't want rain," Bake said to someone with him. "Rain will help them more than it will help us."

In the dining room of the motel, Dr. James Nicholas, who had operated on Joe's knees so often, was talking with André Kostelanetz, the famous conductor. The maestro had come there as Dr. Nicholas' guest to see the game the next day.

Joe came by their table. Dr. Nicholas introduced Joe to the maestro.

"Tomorrow," said the maestro, smiling, "it's the grand finale for you."

Joe smiled. The maestro was correct. Tomorrow was the grand finale, the final game, the ultimate game, the game that would decide the championship of pro football.

"You're right, it's the end for us and for the Colts," Joe said. "And what a surprise ending it's going to be."

"You did it, boy...."

THE JET PLAYERS sat at the the tables, which were covered with white tablecloths. On the tables were pitchers of orange juice and milk. Waiters brought steaming trays of eggs, pancakes, chopped steak or sirloin steak.

The Jets were being served their pregame meal. The time was eleven o'clock in the morning, January 12, 1969. The Super Bowl was only four hours away. In the hotel dining room, all was quiet except for the clatter of silverware and the low murmur of conversation. No one was very hungry. Butterflies fluttered inside most of the players. Joe cut into a steak. He tasted a piece, chewing it slowly.

He sliced off another piece, picked it up with his fork, then set it down. He reached over with a spoon, dipping it into a jar of honey. He swallowed a few teaspoonfuls of honey. He couldn't eat anything else.

Other players pushed back their chairs from the tables, their food hardly touched. Most were quiet, thinking of the game. Each player hoped he wouldn't make a mistake — a mistake that would cost the Jets the victory. Besides costing each man the first-prize money of $15,000, and the team a whole season's work, it could cost the Jets and the AFL a championship.

At a little before noon the players filed out of the motel into two buses. The buses moved slowly out to the highway toward Miami, then braked to a stop.

Now three other buses pulled in behind the two Jets' buses. These were carrying the Colts, who had been staying at a nearby hotel. Cops on motorcycles roared ahead of the first bus and waved to the drivers to follow. With sirens wailing, motorcycles and buses raced down Route A1A toward Miami and the Orange Bowl, the scene of Super Bowl 3.

The Jet players were quiet as they whizzed

along, most staring out the window at palm trees. Joe was in the first bus. The driver of Joe's bus spoke into a microphone. "We've got the Colts behind us," he said. "Let's keep it that way all day."

The Jet players laughed and burst into applause. But soon they were quiet again, thinking about the game. Joe stared out the window. He saw the sun slipping behind scudding gray clouds. It would be a cool, partly cloudy day, making for a dry field.

As though Joe were watching a movie, a scene began to form in front of his eyes. He saw Don Maynard racing down the sideline. He saw himself lean back and arch a long pass. And then he saw Maynard catch the ball and run into the end zone for a touchdown.

The scene dissolved. A new scene began in front of Joe's eyes. He saw himself calling signals. He saw a Colt safety man blitzing toward him. He saw himself take the snap, straighten up, and throw a pass to a Jet receiver in the area left open by the blitzer. Beautiful, Joe thought, beautiful.

"There it is," barked the voice of Jet back Mark Smolinski, breaking the silence. "Here we are."

The players saw the hulking Orange Bowl.

They saw lines of fans streaming toward the entrances. The buses lumbered toward the players' gate. When the Jets' two buses swayed to a stop, fans crowded around the doors, shouting, "We want Namath, we want Namath...."

"Joe, you'd better get off first," called out Pete Lammons, the tight end. "Otherwise nobody on this bus will be able to get off in time for the kickoff."

Joe, smiling, stepped out of the bus. The Jet fans cheered and pounded him on the back. His head down, Joe moved quickly through the crowd and into the stadium. The Jet players followed behind their quarterback.

Inside the clubhouse the Jets pulled on white jerseys with green numerals. Trainers were wrapping adhesive tape around players' ankles. Joe was stretched out on a table as trainer Jeff Snedeker carefully wrapped the quarterback's delicate right knee. Snedeker fixed an aluminum and black rubber brace to the knee, taping it tightly.

Joe's leg was almost as rigid as a pole. He could not get off the table. Snedeker gripped Joe by the waist and lowered him to the floor.

Joe stomped off toward his locker, the right leg peg-leg stiff.

A priest stopped Joe. "What should I pray for, Joe?" the priest asked.

"Pray that nobody gets hurt," Joe said.

The room was very quiet as the players finished dressing. They sat in twos and threes, murmuring in low voices, going over last-minute plans.

Coach Weeb Ewbank came into the room. He spoke for a few minutes, telling his players one last time how important this game would be to them for all their lives. Then the players knelt, each player holding the hands of teammates on both sides of him. Paul Crane, the big linebacker, recited "The Lord's Prayer." When he finished, the players rose and started for the door, heads down, helmets in hand.

"One last thing!" Coach Ewbank yelled.

The players stopped. "When we win," Ewbank shouted, grinning, "don't anybody pick me up on their shoulders. I'll walk."

The Jets laughed, then cheered. Their cleats clattered on the cement floor as they trotted through a tunnel. They came out of the tunnel onto the playing field of the Orange Bowl. They felt a cool breeze blowing

Joe drops back to pass in 1969 Super Bowl game at Miami.

into their faces as they ran to the sideline, and the roaring of some 75,000 fans cascading down onto the field. Across the nation some sixty million TV watchers stared intently at their screens.

The Colts kicked off to the Jets, who returned the ball to the New York 23-yard line. The offensive unit, led by Joe, trotted onto the field. In the huddle Joe barked, "OK, nineteen straight. On three."

The Jets clapped hands and wheeled smartly out of their huddle. Joe snapped out signals which told the Jets to shift. Left guard Bob Talamini moved between the center and the right guard. Joe saw the Colt defense moving to meet the shift.

Good. Joe wanted the Colts to know the Jets would use this shift. It could confuse the Colts. Joe wanted them to know they weren't playing against a bunch of kids. They were playing against the champions of the American Football League.

Joe took the snap. He handed off to Matt Snell, who bulled through the line for three yards. In the huddle Joe again called for the nineteen-straight play. This time Snell followed behind the blocking of 300-pound Winston Hill, who bounced Colt tackle Ordell

Braase out of the way. Snell ran for nine yards and a first down.

Now Joe knew the Jets could run against the Colt line, especially against Braase. Winston Hill was younger and stronger than Braase.

Joe called for a pass. He wondered if the Colts would blitz.

Joe stepped back. Sure enough, he saw a linebacker blitzing. Joe saw Matt Snell burst into the area left open by the blitzer. Joe threw to Snell who caught the pass for a nine-yard gain. Just as Joe had suspected, he could complete short passes against the Baltimore blitz.

However, the Jets had to punt. The Colts took the ball on their 27 and immediately muscled their way toward the Jet goal line. Their quarterback, Earl Morrall, threw a pass to tight end John Mackey who trampled over Jet linebacker Jim Hudson and ran for a nineteen-yard gain. Morrall handed off to his backs who smashed up the middle and ripped around the ends. Suddenly the Colts were on the Jet 19.

Here the Jet defense stiffened. The Colts sent in Lou Michaels, Joe's old pal, to try to kick a field goal. The pudgy Lou stepped forward and booted the ball. It soared toward the goalposts, then faded away. The referee signaled the kick was no good.

The Jets took the ball on their 20. Joe threw to Bill Mathis for a first down on the 35. Looking at the Colt defense, Joe decided to try the play he had seen in the "movie" he'd watched on the bus. He told Don Maynard to streak down the sideline on a "bomb" pattern.

Joe took the ball, cocked it. He threw. The ball soared downfield. Maynard turned and saw the ball arching down toward him. He stretched out his hands. The ball sailed within inches of his fingers and dropped to the grass.

Joe saw the ball bouncing along the grass. He put his hands on his hips, disappointed. This wasn't the ending he'd seen in the "movie." But there would be other chances.

Maynard trotted back toward the Jet huddle, limping. "Don has an injured leg," said Weeb Ewbank at the sideline. "If his leg was all right, he would have caught that ball for a touchdown."

A few plays later George Sauer snared a pass from Joe at the New York 12. A Colt slammed into Sauer. The ball popped out of his hands. Another Colt plopped onto the fumble. The Colts had the ball only twelve yards away from a touchdown.

Again the Jet defense rose up strong. The Colt runners could not score. Earl Morrall threw a pass into the end zone. A Jet reached up and tipped the ball. The ball hit a Colt's shoulder and hopped high into the air. The Jets' Randy Beverly leaped and grabbed the ball. The Jets had intercepted! Again they had stopped the Colts from scoring.

The Jets took over with the ball on the 20. Now Joe knew all he needed to know about the Colt defense. He knew what plays would work. But the Colts were changing their defenses after Joe called each play in the huddle. Joe told the Jets, "I'll start calling most of the plays at the line. Check with me."

Standing over his center, Joe scanned the defense. He looked for the weak points. He called signals. Each Jet had to listen attentively while the crowd roared. If one player missed a word, a color like "red" or "blue," or a number, the play would collapse. Not once did the Jets mess up a play.

The Jets slammed seventy-six yards to the Colt four. Joe saw Lou Michaels trot onto the field to replace Ordell Braase at tackle. Joe knew that with the bulky Michaels in the game, the Colts would be in a tight five-one defense. From all those hours of looking at movies, Joe knew that the Colts never switched out of that defense, so he could call the play in the huddle.

Joe stepped into the huddle. "Nineteen straight," he told the Jets. "And we'll go on the first sound."

The Jets clapped hands and broke out of the huddle. Joe walked quickly to the line. He put his cupped hands under John Schmitt. He did not dare even clear his throat. At the first sound from him, the Jets would charge off the line of scrimmage. Joe hoped that sudden charge would surprise the Colts.

Joe looked to his right. He looked to his left. The Jets were set.

"Now!" he yelled. The Jet line charged into the Colts. Joe took the snap and handed the ball to Snell. The big back burst through a hole in the line and galloped into the end zone. The Jets led 6-0. It was the first time in the history of the Super Bowl that an AFL team had led.

Jim Turner kicked the extra point and the Jets trooped off the field at the half ahead, 7-0. In the clubhouse, as Joe was gulping down a Coke, Coach Ewbank took him aside. "We don't want to sit on the lead," Weeb said. "Let's assume we're seven points behind instead of seven points ahead. We want to keep driving."

"Right!" Joe said.

In the third period the Jets kept on driving, pushing to the Colt 25. From there Jim Turner kicked a field goal. The Jets led, 10-0.

A little later the Jets marched to the Baltimore 32. Joe stepped back to pass. He threw the ball. A Colt pass rusher rammed into Joe and Joe felt pain shoot up his right arm.

Bent over, Joe hobbled off the field, signaling for number-two quarterback Babe Parilli to take his place. A finger of Joe's throwing hand was numb. A doctor and two trainers hovered over the hand, the doctor ever so carefully trying to fix the finger.

Out on the field, on fourth down, the Jets lined up to try another field goal. Parilli took the snap, placed down the ball. Jim Turner strode forward, kicked, and the ball arched high over the goalposts. The Jets now led, 13-0.

Joe watched from the sideline as Johnny Unitas, his boyhood idol, trotted out to replace Morrall for the Colts. But Johnny U., his arm sore, could not move the Colts. The Colts had to punt.

"I can go in, Weeb," Joe told Ewbank.

"Go ahead," Weeb said.

Jet fans stood and cheered when they saw Joe coming back into the game. This game was not won yet, not with the still-dangerous Unitas pitching passes. And Unitas had plenty of time to pass for two touchdowns and put the Colts ahead. There were more than twenty minutes remaining in the game.

Joe knew that the Jets could use more points, so he went right on attacking the Colt defense. Each time Joe threw to the left, pain flashed through his hand. But Joe threw to Sauer on the left, and Sauer ran to the Colt 49 for the first down.

The Jets gathered in the huddle. "Let's fake the slant-in pattern and go," Sauer said to Joe.

"You got it, George," Joe said. "Fake the slant-in pattern and then take off."

Joe took the ball and dropped backward. He saw Sauer run the slant-in pattern, then suddenly burst past his man, who'd been fooled. Joe threw the ball on a low arc. Sauer reached out and caught the ball in full stride.

He ran all the way to the Colt 10 before a fast defensive back tripped him up from behind.

The Jets rammed to the six. Whistles tooted, signaling the end of the third period. Joe walked to the sideline to talk to Ewbank. "I'm not going to take any chances," Joe said. "I'm just going to get some points on the board. Do you agree with that?"

"I agree with you, Joe. Play your game but don't have any interceptions."

Joe trotted back to join the Jets. He called for two running plays into the line. The Colts held. On fourth down Jim Turner kicked another field goal, this one from the 16-yard line, and the Jets led, 16-0.

Johnny Unitas came onto the field with the Colt offense. His bony face grim, Johnny U. studied the Jet defense with his wise old quarterback's eyes. He called for a run up the middle, then a pass, then another run. From his 20 he steered the Colts eighty yards for a touchdown. New York 16, Baltimore 7.

Joe looked at the clock. Only three minutes remained in the game. Joe called for running plays, using up as much time as possible. Then the Jets punted.

Unitas came out for one more drive. He threw a pass to Tom Matte, who caught the

The Colts' tall Bubba Smith leaps in a vain attempt to block a pass from Namath in the Super Bowl upset at Miami in 1969.

ball and was tackled near the Jet bench. Some of the Jet players yelled insults at Matte.

"Don't do that," Joe said, quieting them. "If we're going to be champions, we're going to have to act like champions."

The canny Unitas threw pass after pass into weak areas of the Jet defense. He moved the Colts to the Jet 19 with only two minutes left in the game. On fourth down he stepped back to pass. He threw. A Colt pass receiver leaped for the ball, but the ball shot by him, the pass incomplete.

Head down, the arm-weary Unitas walked slowly off the field. "I kind of feel sorry for him," a Jet said.

"Don't feel sorry for him," Joe said. "If we'd lost he wouldn't be feeling sorry for you."

The clock showed only a minute to go, the sky darkening now over the Orange Bowl. A low, expectant roar began to rise from the stands, the fans beginning their salute to the Jets for their underdog triumph. The exultant Jets jumped up and down along the sideline, watching the final seconds tick off.

"You told us so," one Jet yelled at Joe.

"I guaranteed it," Joe said, laughing.

The gun sounded. The crowd roared as the

Jets, 16-7 victors, ran off the field. Joe waved one finger high into the air, telling the crowd and the nation watching on TV: The Jets were Number One.

The Jets swarmed into their clubhouse, and Weeb Ewbank ordered the doors locked. He wanted his team together, alone, for one last moment. Johnny Sample, the defensive captain, and Joe Namath, the offensive captain, gripped their hands together as Paul Crane said "The Lord's Prayer," a thanksgiving that no one had been seriously hurt.

Guards flung open the doors. Throngs of reporters and photographers squeezed into the crowded, steamy room. "Where are the NFL writers who picked the Colts to win by eighteen points?" Joe yelled. "I'll only talk to the writers who picked the Jets to win."

The writers grinned, knowing Joe was enjoying one of his put-on jokes. Suddenly Joe saw a slender man in a straw hat working his way through the crowd. The man was crying, the tears spilling down his cheeks. "You did it, boy," yelled Joe Namath's father. "You did it."

That night, back at the Colts' hotel, safety man Rich Volk suddenly fainted. He'd been knocked unconscious twice during the game. An ambulance rushed Volk to a hospital. Doctors discovered he had a mild concussion. He would be all right in a few days, the doctors said.

The next morning a messenger brought flowers to the hospital. "These flowers are for you," a nurse told Rich Volk, giving the flowers to him.

Volk opened an envelope pinned to the flowers. Inside was a card wishing him a speedy recovery. The card was signed by Joe Namath.

Joe Comes Home

THE LONG LINE of limousines cruised down the highway. In the back seat of one limousine sat Joe Namath. Next to Joe was his high school football coach, Larry Bruno. On the other side of Joe sat his father.

The limousines had met Joe at the Pittsburgh airport. Now they were taking Joe to Beaver Falls, where his friends were celebrating Joe Namath Day. It was a sunny May day in 1969, a few months after the triumph by the Jets in the Super Bowl. "You really showed the Colts what you could do," Larry Bruno was saying.

"All the Jets showed the Colts what we could do," Joe said, smiling.

The limousines rolled across the bridge over the Beaver River. Joe leaned forward in the limousine to look at the railroad trestle over the river. He remembered that day when he and his friend, Linwood Alford, had been trapped on the trestle.

The limousines drove slowly into Beaver Falls. They stopped at a parking lot. Joe got out of the limousine and climbed into an open car. Don Maynard, Johnny Sample, and George Sauer stepped into other open cars behind the car carrying Joe.

With police cars blinking their red lights, the parade of cars turned slowly onto Sixth Street in the Lower End, where Joe had grown up. Joe, perched atop a seat, saw the two-story white frame house in which he'd lived as a boy. He remembered the many cold mornings when he had hated to get out of bed because the house was so frigid.

The cars turned onto Seventh Avenue and Joe saw people massed on the sidewalks. He stared, amazed. Everyone in town must be here. Everyone in the *Valley* must be here. Police estimated the crowd at 25,000, twice the population of Beaver Falls. Children raced off the sidewalk and rushed up to Joe's car, reaching out their hands to shake his.

145

Joe leaned down and shook hands, grinning and laughing.

He saw his mother. She was standing with friends. The cars stopped. She came over and kissed Joe. Everyone cheered. The pride of Beaver Falls had come home.

That evening more than a thousand people filled the field house at Geneva College to attend a banquet for Joe. Signs were plastered on the walls. "Thanks, Joe, for putting us on the map." "Welcome Home, Joe." "We Love You, Joe." Photos of Joe looked down on the tables — photos of Joe in high school, in college, as a Jet.

Joe was sitting at the head table. He saw his mother at a nearby table dabbing her eyes. She felt very proud. His father was talking happily with friends. The people of Beaver Falls stared at Joe. They remembered the kid they once called Joey U. Now he was the famous Joe Namath, one of the most famous football players in the nation.

His teammates, his coach, Weeb Ewbank, and his friends rose to speak of Joe and his great performance in the Super Bowl. The former Beaver Falls High School football coach, Bill Ross, told how he had failed to invite Joe to a training camp for the football team. "I was a great judge of talent," Ross joked, smiling, and everyone laughed.

Then it was Joe's turn to speak. He walked slowly to the microphone in his slouched way. He hunched over slightly as he spoke into the microphone and his words echoed from the loudspeakers in the hushed hall:

"I want to thank my parents, my brothers, my coaches, and all my teammates. They all helped form my skill. Without them I couldn't have accomplished anything. Eventually I hope to come back here some day and settle down. . . ."

The people of Beaver Falls applauded. They wanted Joe to come back.

A month later it seemed that Joe might come back to Beaver Falls sooner than he had expected. Joe announced his retirement from pro football, shocking fans everywhere. NFL commissioner Pete Rozelle had ordered Joe to sell his share of a New York restaurant called Bachelors III. Commissioner Rozelle said that gamblers had dined in the place. Joe said a lot of people came into the restaurant. It was a public place. He said he was quitting football rather than sell the restaurant. "It's a matter of principle," Joe said in a televised interview at the restaurant. He couldn't hold back his tears.

Joe flew to Hollywood, where he played the part of a Marine in a movie titled *Norwood*. Film producers signed him to make two more movies. He liked making movies. He went out on dates with beautiful girls, he bought fancy new clothes, and he was being paid $60,000 for only two weeks of filming. Who needed pro football?

The Jet players knew they needed Joe. That summer they gathered at their preseason camp at Hofstra. Sitting in the dormitories, they talked of their missing leader. "One thing's for sure," said Gerry Philbin. "We won't win without him."

"Joe has to do what he thinks is right," George Sauer said. "I told people I'd quit if Joe quit. Now I realize I was wrong. I have to do what is right for me, just as Joe has to do what he thinks is right."

Joe flew back to New York to confer with Commissioner Rozelle. They met in the commissioner's office high above Rockefeller Center. Rozelle told Joe that a football star must be like a Supreme Court Justice: above suspicion. If people saw Joe with a crook, they could say, "If Joe travels with crooks, then Joe also must be a crook."

Joe argued that he was seen with hundreds of people every day. Men and women ran up to him and asked for his autograph. He didn't know their names. He couldn't possibly know if they were saints or crooks.

Finally Rozelle and Joe agreed: He would sell his share of the Bachelors III restaurant in New York. But he could keep the Bachelor III restaurants he owned in other cities. And Joe would come back to football.

Joe and Rozelle shook hands. "I'd be a fool if I didn't want to see you back in football," the commissioner told Joe. "You are the biggest name we have."

Joe smiled and thanked the commissioner. "Oh, Joe," Rozelle said. "Could you sign these photos?"

The commissioner handed Joe two photographs. Joe looked at them. They were photos of Joe Namath. "I'd like you to sign them for my daughter," the commissioner said. "She's a big fan of yours."

Joe happily signed the photos. The commissioner would give the photos to his daughter. That proved to Joe that the commissioner knew he had done nothing wrong. Joe rejoined the Jets for the start of the 1969 season.

The team won nine of its last eleven games to win the AFL's Eastern Division championship for the second straight season. The Jets faced Kansas City in the playoffs for the AFL championship. With Kansas City leading, 13-6, and only a minute left in the game, Joe fired pass after pass into the hands of his receivers. The Jets drove to the one-foot line, only twelve inches separating them from victory and the chance to go to their second straight Super Bowl.

The Chiefs threw back the Jets, time ran out, and Kansas City won, 13-6. In the winners' clubhouse Chief coach Hank Stram wiped his sweaty forehead and told reporters, "When you play against Namath, you can never be sure you've won until you're in the clubhouse."

In that 1969 season the Jet players named Joe their Most Valuable Player for the second consecutive year. And the AFL coaches selected Joe as the league's Most Valuable Player and best passer.

At the start of the 1970 season many sportswriters were predicting a first-place finish for the Jets. Early in the season Joe

Joe lands on his wrist which he would injure more severely later in this 1970 game which the Jets lost to the Colts.

stepped back to pass. A tackler dived at him, one hand cracking Joe across the right wrist. Joe threw the ball, then gripped the wrist, biting his lips. A dull ache was spreading across it. After the game doctors discovered a broken bone in the wrist.

For the rest of the season Joe watched from the sideline as young quarterback Al Woodall tried to lead the Jets. But Woodall made mistakes and the Jets won only four games in 1970 while losing ten. Joe paced the sideline, as fit and strong as he had ever been. Yet he couldn't do the one thing a quarterback must be able to do: He couldn't throw.

"He's eating his heart out," defensive end Gerry Philbin said one day. "He sees a defense and knows he can pass for touchdowns against a defense like that. But he can't throw. It's driving him crazy."

At the start of the 1971 season Joe reported to camp with the button-eyed enthusiasm of a rookie. He was usually the first one to trot out for practice in the morning, among the last to walk off in the afternoon. Center John Schmitt said to him one day, "Joe, I've never seen you work harder in practice."

Joe looked at Schmitt. "John, last year I really learned something," Joe said.

"What do you mean?"

"I learned how much football means to me. Last year I was having fun making movies. I was getting a kick out of appearing on TV shows. There were the Bachelor III restaurants opening up all across the country. I thought: Boy, this show-business life is great. Who needs football? Then I got hurt and couldn't play. I had to stand there and watch someone else be the Jets' quarterback. I found out how much I need football. I've been playing it too long to quit now. I'm only twenty-eight years old. I want to go on playing for another seven or eight years."

John Schmitt nodded. "You'll be playing until you're ninety the way you're throwing," John said. "I've never seen you throwing harder."

A few days later the Jets flew south to play the Detroit Lions in a preseason game at Tampa, Florida. Late in the first half a Jet fumbled the ball. Detroit linebacker Mike Lucci picked up the ball and sped down the sideline.

Joe ran over to stop him. This was a meaningless exhibition game but Joe was a foot-

Joe Namath against the Buffalo Bills: He made these meaningless games exciting.

ball player. He dived to tackle Lucci. He missed and a Detroit blocker fell on Joe's left knee. Lucci dashed into the end zone for a touchdown.

Joe got up slowly. "Are you all right?" the Detroit blocker asked him.

"I'm OK," Joe said with a grin. "I guess this just proves I'm no defensive back."

Joe started to walk off the field. The left knee felt strange under him. At the sideline Dr. Nicholas examined the knee, which was already puffing. He looked up at Joe and Joe knew what the doctor was going to say: He would need another operation.

The next day, back in New York, Dr. Nicholas operated, repairing damaged ligaments. It looked as though Joe were through for the season. Instead he came back halfway through to toss those three touchdown passes against San Francisco, rallying the Jets from a 24-7 beating to a narrow 24-21 defeat.

That season Joe completed 50 percent of his passes. And now he was an idol wherever the Jets played. The team flew to San Diego for a game. Jet officials said Joe would not play — and he didn't. But after the game some 5,000 fans encircled the Jet clubhouse, clamoring to see Joe. When he came out, they roared.

In almost every city fans mobbed the Jet buses, screaming for Joe. "Wherever we go," said lineman Dave Herman, "all you hear is, 'Where's Joe?' ... 'We want Joe!' Sometimes I'm afraid they'll tear down the bus just to get at Joe."

When Joe was able to play late in 1971, the Jets were hopelessly out of the race. So were teams like Buffalo, New England, and Cincinnati. But when the Jets played New England or Buffalo, Joe made these meaningless games exciting. "You can be ahead of Joe and the Jets by two touchdowns with five minutes to go," said Buffalo official Jack Horrigan, "and Joe will have you quaking in your boots. You know he can throw three touchdowns in five minutes."

Before the start of the 1972 season, fans were talking about what pro football would be like without Joe Namath. His knees pained Joe. Although he was only twenty-nine, there were rumors he would retire. His friend, TV sportscaster Dick Schaap, summed up what he thought pro football would be like without Joe. "The game will go on," Schaap said.

John Wayne's son is introduced to Joe on the set of *Rio Lobo*.

"But for a while the game won't be as much fun."

Joe didn't want to quit. In the spring of 1972 he was talking to a friend. "If I had my way," he said, "I'd like to spend every autumn of my life throwing passes. When you throw a fifty-yard pass, you feel as if there's nothing in sports that can be more exciting. I can see where pro football is tough on linemen and running backs. They take a lot of punishment. But it's fun being a quarterback and a passer."

Joe, however, had to think about what he would do when he left football. After having made three movies and appeared on TV shows with Johnny Carson, Dick Cavett, Dean Martin, and other celebrities, Joe was already a star in show business.

With dozens of the most famous movie stars, Joe attended Hollywood's biggest show, the presentation of the 1972 Oscar awards. Joe was called on stage to present an Oscar to the best fashion designer.

Joe grinned as he faced the TV cameras. "I'm number 12 and I play with the New York Jets," Joe said with a grin. "My name is Joe Namath. I don't know much about fashion so I can use all the help I can get."

At that, to Joe's delight, a pretty actress came on stage to help. And when the presentation was over, the audience burst into applause for their favorite quarterback, Joe Namath.

Jet lineman Dave Herman was watching the Oscar show on his TV set. "Look at Joe," Dave said to his wife. "He's up there with the biggest stars of show business. And he's doing just as good a job as any of them."

Mike Bite, Joe's old friend and lawyer, was watching the show in Birmingham, Alabama. "I'll tell you this about Joe," Mike Bite said. "Whatever Joe Namath wants to do, Joe Namath can do. Joe Namath can do *anything!*"

For a while, though, in 1972, it looked as if Joe Namath wouldn't do the one thing he enjoyed most — play football. Joe and the Jets couldn't agree on a contract. Finally, in August 1972, he signed a two-year Jet contract for a reported half a million dollars. Joe became one of the highest paid players in pro football history, but both the Jets and Joe were happy. Joe, the heart and head of the Jets' team, was playing and would be drawing record crowds to the Jets' games for at least a few more seasons.

JOE NAMATH'S RECORD
for the New York Jets

Year	Attempts	Completions	Yards	Interceptions	Touchdowns	Longest Gain	Percentage
1965	340	164	2220	15	18	62	.482
1966	471	232	3379	27	19	77	.493
1967	491	258	4007	28	26	75	.525
1968	380	187	3147	17	15	87	.492
1969	361	185	2734	17	19	60	.512
1970*	179	90	1259	12	5	72	.503
1971††	59	28	537	6	5	74	.474
Totals	2281	1144	17,283	122	107		.501

* Missed nine games because of broken wrist.
†† Missed ten games because of knee operation.

Super Bowl 3
Against Baltimore at Miami

Date	Attempts	Completions	Yards	Interceptions	Touchdowns	Longest Gain	Percentage
Jan. 12, 1969	28	17	206	0	0	41	.607